ACCEPT NO TRASH TALK

Overcoming the Odds

Second Edition

TRACI LAWRENCE

ACCEPT NO TRASH TALK

Copyright © 2014 by Traci Lawrence

Second Edition

This book or any portion thereof may not be reproduced or used in any manner whatsoever, without the express written permission of the author, except for the use of brief quotations in a book review.

This book is licensed for your personal enjoyment only. It may not be re-sold or given away to other people. If you would like to share this book with another person, please purchase an additional copy for each recipient. If you're reading this book and did not purchase it, or it was not purchased for your use only, then please return to your favorite book retailer and purchase your own copy. Thank you for respecting the hard work of this author.

For information, you may contact the author at

tracialawrence@gmail.com

Interior and Cover design by The Book Khaleesi

www.thebookkhaleesi.com

TABLE OF CONTENTS

PREFACE, p. i

INTRODUCTION, p. v

Chapter 1 Rising above Low Expectations: Overcoming, p. 1

Chapter 2 The Healing Power of Positive Change, p. 10

Chapter 3 Excuses That Aggressors Use, p. 16

Chapter 4 The Power of Positive Feedback, p. 34

Chapter 5 The Need for Respect in Relationships, p. 40

Chapter 6 The Importance of Open Communication, p. 56

Chapter 7 The Importance of Rejecting Labels and Stereotypes, p. 62

Chapter 8 How to Diffuse a Trash Talk Situation, p. 69

Chapter 9 Why We Need to Set Up Emotional Boundaries, p. 83

Chapter 10 How to Set Up Emotional Boundaries, p. 88

Chapter 11 Conclusion, p. 91

ACKNOWLEDGEMENTS, p. 101

ABOUT THE AUTHOR, p. 102

PREFACE

ONE NEVER KNOWS what a person can accomplish if they are allowed to live and flourish within their own truth and capabilities. Every individual has value. Every individual has something to offer the world. Unfortunately, certain groups of people seem to reserve the right to decide whose voices will be heard and respected. I chose to write a book that addresses the emotional needs of people who may feel devalued by people and circumstances beyond their control.

There are many excellent self-help books out there. Many of them are written by learned people with a solid pedigree grounded in academia, religion, celebrity status, public speaking, or a combination of the above. I thought it was time for an everyday person who had been marginalized in certain areas of her own life to address a basic concern of every person: persevering in the fight for acceptance. I wanted to do this in a way that would be accessible to people of any faith, ethnicity, and socio-economic level.

Psychology tells us that the need for acceptance transcends all physical and mental borders and labels. If we're human, we want to belong. It's that simple. We all want to be accepted. Unfortunately, we don't always get accepted. That's the area in which my book may be of assistance.

Why My Book Is Different

MY BOOK IS DIFFERENT from other books because its author is different from other authors. I am not an esteemed celebrity. Along the same lines, I am not an academic with seven to ten letters behind my name whose knowledge of the subject matter is rooted in elite textbooks or classrooms.

Simply put, this is a straightforward book about the need to keep negative thoughts and voices out of our lives. It's an emotionally cold world out there. The trauma keeps getting closer and closer to home as the internet connects everybody to everywhere–in real time. We are more likely than ever to encounter people who take issue with the way we talk, the way we think, the way we look, the way we act, and our value system.

It has become nearly impossible to please all of the people all of the time. Therefore, it has become more important than ever to follow the light within ourselves, not the negativity that is so prevalent everywhere.

The reason that this book will be helpful to the reader is that I, the author, can relate wholeheartedly to anybody who has been marginalized. Most of my life, I have been labeled as "different". Here are a few of my variations from "the norm" in a nutshell: I am an adult, but I am the size of some 9-year olds; I am a member of a marginalized Christian denomination; I am socially awkward; and, I have some uncommon medical and mental concerns.

Why I Have Been Marginalized

My Height

THERE ARE MANY REASONS why a person might be marginalized. Yet, my personal experience is that my uncommon size is one of the main reasons I have been harassed. Height, or large size, is often considered to be equal to dominance in nature.

The principle of height equaling dominance also translates over to some human societies, especially in traditionally tall western societies. Throughout history, smaller people have been disrespected across the board in the United States, especially through the mid-20th century. Two illustrations of this are found in the Munchkins of *The Wizard of Oz* and the Oompa Loompas of *Willie Wonka and The Chocolate Factory*.

The fact that we still allow Hollywood to set standards that lead people to mistreat their bodies and spend thousands of dollars on altering their appearance begs the question: why should we let one group of people dictate how we should look, think, and act? Who made them the arbiters of "normal"? People do not come in only one shape and size, and that's a good thing!

My Slow-Paced Personality

THE SECOND REASON I have been disrespected is my slow-paced personality. The United States is a country full of fast-paced, impatient people. The dominant personality in the country seems to be the A-Type, controlling, personality. People of this type act and think quickly. On the other hand, people who have a personality that is more slow-paced and analytical can be overlooked and marginalized. Such an attitude can be a liability because some jobs require a person to be analytical and thorough.

My chronic medical problems relate to gluten sensitivity. Gluten sensitivity, or intolerance, refers to an autoimmune disorder. When a person that is sensitive to gluten—a protein found mainly in rye, wheat, and barley—eats gluten, their body makes antibodies to the gluten. The antibodies treat the gluten as a foreign object and attack it. This can damage the intestinal system. Because I ate gluten for decades before I got diagnosed with gluten intolerance, many of my organs and systems have been compromised, including my brain.

The main way gluten affected my brain was that it clouded my thinking. This cloudy thinking made me socially awkward. Therefore, I have often been disrespected. Even people who were close to me have assumed they had a right to judge me because I didn't act, look, or think like them.

The Purpose of the Book

THIS BOOK IS MEANT to empower anybody who feels marginalized to push beyond the borders of their own marginalization.

The two main points of this book are the following:

- Every individual has unique challenges, even the strongest among us.
- It's possible for anyone to push through their struggles.

Of necessity, this book will use examples from my own life and research. (I will not use the real names of the everyday people whose stories I relate.) However, this is not a book just about me; it's a book for all undervalued individuals. It's meant to foster solidarity in, and give a voice to, people who have been made to feel inferior.

In order to stay sane, we must all believe we can chop our individual challenges down to size. We can finish the race of life together! Professional athletes usually try not to let injuries stop them from playing out a game, or finishing a race; neither should we. It doesn't matter if we run or walk. What's important is that we stay in the game!

INTRODUCTION

WHAT IS NORMAL? Who has the right to define what is normal? Does one social clique have the right to define normality for a whole group of people? Does any layperson outside of the practitioners of law, law enforcement, or medicine, have the right to appoint themselves an arbiter of normality? I have recently realized that everybody is far from perfect and "normal" can be relative. What's normal to the people of one group may not seem normal to the people of a different group:

- ***The Beverly Hillbillies*** - is a TV situation comedy that first ran in the 1960's. The show chronicles the misadventures of the Clampett family. The Clampetts are a formerly dirt-poor family that moved from a one-room log cabin in Tennessee, United States, to a mansion in Beverly Hills, California, United States. The reason they could afford to move to the Hollywood area is because oil was discovered on their property.

  This hillbilly family that used to live in a tiny log cabin that had no running water or electricity suddenly found themselves living among society's elite. The hillbillies are exposed to new food, clothing, values, interests, modern conveniences, architecture, and patterns of speech. Obviously, the hillbillies are an anomaly to the residents of Beverly Hills, and the residents of Beverly Hills are an anomaly to the hillbillies. Who's right and who's wrong? Does there have to be a right and a wrong? It could be argued that there are advantages and disadvantages to both a simple country life and life in a high-society atmosphere.

  The series is a fictional account, an extreme case, of the ongoing clash between two diametrically opposed cultures. Yet, how many millions of minor examples of such conflicts might be found daily in real life as individuals get exposed to new lifestyles?

- ***Wife Swap*** - is a reality TV series. In this show, the wives of two divergent families trade homes and lifestyles for two weeks. For instance, in one episode, Beth, the matriarch of an obsessively clean household moved into a house where cleaning was rarely done and dozens of pets were allowed to roam free inside the house.

  On each episode of the show, both sides represent excesses. However, the families that participate in the series, those that are humble, often come away from the experience having learned some valuable lessons in making their own lives easier. The most teachable participants in the series learn the important life truth that participating in the extreme of anything can become self-damaging and limiting.

This brings us full circle back to the beginning question of the book's introduction: What is normal? Do the minority of people who live in extremes have a right to define what's normal for the majority of people? On a more basic level, how do we universally define what is normal, aside from defining criminal and ethical behavior? Again, we seem to return to the sovereign individual opinion.

I have come to the healthy realization we weren't put on this earth to judge each other. We're here to help each other, when feasible. We are not all made from the same cookie cutter, and that's a good thing. If all the people on Earth were exactly the same, how would we fill every job? How would we balance each other out, and help each other, if none of us could get beyond our own narrow worlds? Major crises, for example, require a comprehensive thought process to solve.

If everybody looked the same, acted the same, and their thought processes were the same, how would some special people dare to break away from the fold? Where would we find the great inventors, entrepreneurs, entertainers, or groundbreakers of some other sort? Where would the Einsteins, Curies, and Helen Kellers be? These people were all groundbreakers. These people could not be forced into a mold. They broke the mold.

I count it a blessing that people come in different shapes, sizes, colors and personality types. If everyone was a thinker, when would the action get done? On the other hand, if everybody was a person of action, how reliable would our plans and projects be? Our differences contribute to a more sturdy society.

We All Deserve a Better Life

BEFORE WE MOVE ON to the body of the book, let me write a very important disclaimer: This book is not going to touch on the choices that people make daily in regards to ethics, religion, or politics. For example, this book is not going to directly address behavior some people may categorize as immoral or criminal. The object of this book is to use my own life experience and research to empower the average law-abiding, caring, hard-working person to have more faith in his own abilities. I want to help disrespected people rethink the way they allow selfish, or malevolent, people to treat them.

Yes, I'm saying that we do "allow" ourselves to be mistreated in many cases. We all need to learn to fend off the superficial labels and judgments that selfish bullies at all levels of society want to pin on us. It doesn't matter if these bullies have religious reasons, political reasons, or purely selfish reasons for harassing us. They aren't our judges.

This book is especially meant to empower people who are living in a demeaning loop of feeling they aren't "good enough". There are people out there who are conditioned by their circumstances to accept the unpalatable status quo because life has taught them they aren't worthy to expect anything better.

This is not an uncommon feeling among abused people. Victims of severe abuse may give up all hope of living a fulfilling life. They see no need to leave a toxic environment and toxic relationships because they feel there is no alternative to toxicity.

Chapter 1

Rising above Low Expectations: Overcoming

LET ME BEGIN THIS chapter with an important disclaimer: I am not advocating that we ignore our conscience, the basic arbiter of what's right and wrong within each of us. It's important that, if our conscience calls for change, we act accordingly. I'm just saying (irrespective of unethical, criminal, or inappropriate behavior) we shouldn't allow a flow of unabated negative self-talk into our minds.

It's often said each person is their own worst critic. Certain personality types are particularly prone to depression and negativity. These individuals are likely to remember their own failures more than they remember their successes.

Like many people who push beyond ordinary lives, I have "failed" many times. Yet, I keep picking myself back up. I do this by analyzing what I can learn from my failures and pressing on toward my next goal.

More than one powerful person has said true success is built on failure because we learn from our blunders. Mistakes are our real-world classroom. I would venture to say every effective individual has a story of how they overcame tremendous odds on their way to the top. In addition, every follower of history can quote examples of how such luminaries as Thomas Edison, Albert Einstein, Martin Luther King, and Harriet Beecher Stowe overcame many challenges on their way to becoming towering figures in history.

In the same way, currently famous celebrities weren't always well known. It's a documented fact many an A-Lister has had to push beyond addictions, or push beyond the "You'll never be more than a starving artist." stage.

- **Dolly Parton and Naomi Judd** - are legendary Country vocal artists. They both began life modestly in the rural Appalachia area of the United States. In recent decades, these ladies have become country music legends and household names. In fact, both of these women have pushed beyond country music star status: Dolly Parton has starred in numerous movies and TV specials over the decades, and Naomi Judd is a respected author.

- **Tim McGraw** - is another Country vocal artist. He recently decreased his alcohol consumption and embarked on a strenuous fitness routine in order to boost his health. I was uplifted when I read about his new lifestyle, which includes sessions with a fitness trainer. Tim McGraw has completely transformed his body into the body of an athlete.

- **Chris Rock** - is a prominent American comedian. He pulls the bulk of his most well-received material from his childhood. He was bullied when he grew up in an inner-city ghetto. Chris Rock morphed from a sidelined, financially insecure youth into a successful stand-up comedian. In recent years, he has become a Hollywood phenomenon who enjoys guest spots on various talk shows. He even narrates a TV situation comedy based on his youth.

- **Kate Middleton (Her Royal Highness the Duchess of Cambridge)** - married Prince William of the House of Windsor on April 29th, 2011. His Royal Highness, William, Duke of Cambridge, is the grandson of the reigning Queen of England, Elizabeth II. Therefore, he is second-in-line to the throne of England. A British commoner married the world's most eligible bachelor. Another inspirational aspect of this Cinderella story is the fact that she was bullied at both of the boarding schools she attended.

Move Beyond Pity Parties

I, LIKE MANY PEOPLE, can group myself humbly with many prominent figures solely by the fact that I have had to force my mind to think beyond the challenges of my past. I have had to move beyond getting fired from several jobs as well as complications with my health and my relationships.

Anybody can move forward if he chooses to discipline his mind. We have the right to leave the past where it belongs—in the past—and thank it for helping to mold us into the people we are today.

Pity parties get a person nowhere fast, which is something we can learn from any successful person. Nobody makes it to the top of any group, or profession, by living in their past. We have to press on to new territory. Not even an Olympic track athlete could jump over hurdles successfully if he chose to only sit on the ground in front of them and cry. It just doesn't work that way.

We must stay in the race if we want to have a chance of success. We can't climb mountains, or jump over hurdles, by whining and quitting the game. Life is full of metaphorical mountains and hurdles. Effective individuals have forced themselves to grab hold of the belief that their future can be better than their past despite solid evidence to the contrary. Successful people have hope. It takes an amazing amount of hope and determination to reach the top of anything!

- **Helen Keller -** was a prolific American author and guest lecturer. She was struck blind and deaf at the age of 19 months by what is widely presumed to be Scarlet Fever. Apparently, young Helen couldn't conceive of a way to communicate in any civilized manner. It took years of hard work and patience for the dedicated teacher, Annie Sullivan, to connect with the obstreperous young girl whose inability to communicate in the traditional manner had given birth to a deep-seated anger.

Eventually, Helen Keller broke all traditional barriers to communication by learning Braille, reading peoples' lips with her hands, and communicating in sign language on individuals' hands. She not only had superior reading and writing skills, she was a political activist and advocate for people with disabilities. One of her most impressive achievements was the fact that she was the first deaf and blind person to receive a Bachelor of Arts degree from Radcliffe University.

Most people do not face quite so many challenges in their lives. Many individuals are only faced with a variety of temporary hurdles during their lives. How many people would have the stamina to stay in the race if running the race was so constantly exhausting? My guess is that even fewer people would stay in the race if winning the race was a greater longshot than any in Kentucky Derby history.

People like Helen Keller teach us to believe in the future, to believe in ourselves, and to make lemonade out of lemons. I doubt Helen Keller indulged in pity parties, although few people would have more of an excuse to do so.

- **Richie Parker -** is a current YouTube sensation. He was born with no arms. Yet, he hasn't let that deter him from achieving more than many people who have full use of all of their limbs. This amazing young man designs official NASCAR components by manipulating a computer keyboard with his feet. He also designed modifications to his own 1964 Chevrolet Impala SS car. These expert modifications allow him to drive with his feet and shift with his head.

I believe that everyone has their own unique set of challenges. I also trust that each person's trials are tailor made to be the most difficult, and the most likely to produce growth, for them. We don't reach any goals, or rise to the top of any profession, by hang gliding over the emotional mountains that life puts in our paths. Most of us scale our personal peaks through struggles:

- **Theodore "Teddy" Roosevelt –** "Teddy Bear"... For most people, those two words immediately conjure up images of the iconic children's toy. However, some people may not be aware the toy is named after the 26th President of the United States, Theodore (Teddy) Roosevelt. Roosevelt is a sterling example of how a person can overcome their past. He was characterized as a weak and sickly child. His main medical concerns were poor eyesight, chronic headaches, fever, intestinal distress, and asthma.

His asthma was so severe he was often on the brink of suffocation for weeks at a time. Medical science had not, yet, invented inhalers for asthma. The accepted treatment for asthma, at that time, was stimulants. For example, caffeine and tobacco were believed to open up the lungs. Therefore, young Teddy was given cigars to smoke and strong coffee to drink. The risks of smoking are well known today. The strong coffee didn't help Teddy, either; it made him nauseous.

The lynchpin to Teddy's eventual recovery was his father. His father was strong and wise. He told Teddy that he needed to strengthen his sickly, weak body until it matched the caliber of his brilliant mind. Roosevelt's father built a gym in the Roosevelt family home in order to motivate his son. Roosevelt boxed and lifted weights in the home gym, climbed mountains, and participated in competitive boxing and rowing at Harvard University.

When he was a young adult, Roosevelt's physician told him that he had serious heart problems. The doctor suggested Teddy get a non-stressful desk job somewhere. Teddy responded to this suggestion by climbing the Matterhorn.

As President of the United States, he didn't let a potential assassin's bullet slow him down when he was making a speech. He kept on talking, even after he was shot. Interestingly enough, that bullet was never extracted. Roosevelt lived the rest of his life with the bullet lodged in his body.

Roosevelt had completely transformed his body and mind by the time he became president. He had transformed himself into a soldier, athlete, and statesman. He has not gone down in history as a physically weak child plagued by debilitating, chronic medical problems. Instead, he has gone down in history for his stellar military and political accomplishments.

- **Jackie Robinson -** was the unflappable trailblazer who broke the color barrier in major-league baseball single-handedly. He did this by playing his first game for the all-white Brooklyn Dodgers on April 15th, 1947. He endured an amazing amount of abuse as the first person to break out of the colored league. I saw historical video footage of one of Robinson's first games with the Dodgers. The all-white crowd was loudly jeering him when he first ran into the stadium. However, that same crowd ended up cheering him when they saw a display of this determined man's raw talent. Despite unbelievable opposition, Robinson stayed the course and proved his worth.

Branch Rickey, President and General Manager of the Brooklyn Dodgers, recruited Robinson and supported him. Rickey's unflagging faith in Robinson's ability is probably one of the reasons Jackie Robinson was able to push himself to succeed in a world that had previously been closed to him. He won many honors and titles.

- **Wilma Rudolph** - was an Olympic track star who won three gold medals in the 1960 Rome Olympics. However, few people could have anticipated such a glorious outcome. Wilma Rudolph was an African American fighting for her rights in a time of rampant racial inequality. Also, she had to overcome an amazing amount of physical disabilities. She was born severely premature. She had infantile paralysis, caused by polio. (She had to wear a leg brace and orthopedic shoes for most of her childhood.) In addition, she contracted Scarlet Fever.

- **Alexander Graham Bell** - was a groundbreaking American inventor. At first, his prototype of the telephone wasn't popular. The public mocked the idea. Top scientists didn't see how it was possible for the human voice to carry through wires. Bell's invention was so marginalized it was relegated to an out-of-the-way niche at the 1876 Centennial World's Fair in Philadelphia, Pennsylvania, United States. For weeks, thousands of people, including the fair's judges, passed by the prototype without noticing it.

That all changed when the emperor of Brazil recognized Bell at the fair and asked to be allowed to try his invention. The emperor was suitably impressed. History records that there were numerous inventions displayed at the Centennial Fair. However, the telephone stands out as one of the most remarkable inventions to have been introduced at that time.

- **"Colonel" Harland Sanders** - "KFC"... What fast-food aficionado is unaware of this acronym for Kentucky Fried Chicken, one of the most well-known chicken franchises in the world? Yet, few people had as sluggish a start in life as legendary KFC founder, Harland Sanders of Kentucky, United States. Sanders dropped out of school by the sixth grade so that he could take care of his brothers. He flitted through about a dozen careers in his young adulthood. He even flirted with the idea of becoming a political candidate.

By the age of 40, Sanders had settled down into a career as the owner of a pint-size gas station. He also sold food in this same gas station. In 1935, the state of Kentucky gave Sanders the honorary title of "Colonel" solely to honor his fantastic cooking skills, as first displayed at his small gas station.

Eventually, Saunders' food was attracting more customers to his small business than his gasoline. He was doing a fairly brisk business until a new highway was built that bypassed his business completely. Customers stopped coming. At 65 years old, Sanders went bankrupt.

Luckily for millions of KFC lovers everywhere, the story doesn't end there. Sanders used his first Social Security check to start franchising his chicken recipe. From there, the popularity of his chicken snowballed. He sold his company for $2,000,000 (14.8 million dollars in today's money) in 1964. Currently, KFC serves approximately 12 million customers in more than 15,000 restaurants in 109 countries daily.

Be Thankful For Every Improvement in Your Life

MY PURPOSE IN MENTIONING the life stories of particular celebrities, including their struggles, is to demonstrate to all of us how victories are often gained in baby steps. Colonel Saunders did not go from bankruptcy to selling a 14.8 million-dollar business overnight. Helen Keller didn't go from an angry, uncommunicative young girl to a prolific author, lecturer, and college graduate overnight. Jackie Robinson had to fight rampant racism over a period of years in order to finally win his place in history. Teddy Roosevelt didn't transform his sickly body into that of an athlete overnight. Alexander Graham Bell had to wait patiently for his invention, the telephone, to become appreciated. Wilma Rudolph did not overcome childhood polio in just a few years.

What these people had in common was persistence and a belief in their own capabilities. I'm hoping this book can enable the reader to trust more in his own intuition and capabilities as he embarks on his own path to victory.

For my part, I am not the mentally, physically whole person I hoped to be at this point in my life. On the other hand, I am not the same person I was. I am thankful for the small improvements I see in my life daily. Even if I am just taking baby steps forward, I am still moving forward. I have trained myself to be grateful for what might appear to be small blessings. They can boost a person's confidence level tremendously.

Some examples of small blessings that I've received recently include: unexpected discounts at stores; being led to shows and movies on TV I've been hoping to see; a good book I've been wanting to read; a tasty treat I've been searching for; information that finally addresses a particular concern; a natural, inexpensive remedy for a chronic skin condition, and; money I forgot I had. These are all types of blessings that can help almost any person believe that their life must be improving in some ways, even though their life may still be far from perfect in many ways.

Please pause now to consider what small blessings you have received lately. Has someone shown you unexpected kindness, or gratitude? Did your kids thank you, for once? Did your boss thank you, for once? Have you slept better than you normally do this past week? Did you narrowly avoid an automobile crash? Did you skillfully avoid a road-rage incident? Are you further along on a huge project than expected? Did you have an unanticipated chance to spend time communicating with a loved one? Has a recent purchase been unexpectedly discounted? Have you been led to financial help? Were you able to cross more off your "to do" list than expected? Did someone do you an unexpected favor? Has your health improved in the past week, even a little?

I challenge all of us to constantly keep track of, and be thankful for, even the smallest improvements we see in our own lives. Focusing on what's right in our lives is the surest way to cultivate joy. **Joy can be defined as stability, or contentment, regardless of circumstances.** Focusing solely on what's wrong with our lives is the quickest route to depression. A negative concentration can be disastrous to our health.

I am trying to train myself to be thankful for the simple joys in my life, even though I still have not seen most of the major breakthroughs I had hoped to see. I am much happier now that I have convinced myself I don't need to wait until I've achieved a "major" victory to find joy in everyday life. I can find pleasure in small victories. On the other hand, if I wait until I achieve a huge success to choose to be happy, I may be resigning myself to living without joy for an extended period of time.

Sometimes, it's the small breakthroughs that open the door to life-changing events. We may find that a few small steps forward add up to major advances in a sort of divine mathematical equation. Most of us cannot expect sustained periods of giddy happiness in life. Yet, many people can expect to feel content with even minor successes. At any given moment, there may be more wrong with our life than there is right. Still, we can believe positive change is forthcoming, if we're willing to work for it.

Chapter 2

The Healing Power of Positive Change

WE ALL CHOOSE OUR own level of happiness, or joy. We all make our own choice on how much we will let our past affect our present and future. Just because we were financially challenged, bullied, physically frail, undereducated, socially insecure, underemployed, or generally disrespected earlier in our lives does not mean we must carry these labels with us throughout our entire existence.

Our past does not have to affect our future. No such law exists in the books. Bullies from our childhood may want us to believe we can never change, but that doesn't mean we must live up to (or down to) their low expectations. I have heard it said many times there are two words that should not be in our vocabulary: "never" and "always." The problem is that both of these words seem to discount the possibility of change. Not planning for victory through positive transformation is an example of a wrong mindset.

Even small successes require a combination of talent and hard work over a period of time. For numerous people, even the thought of modification is intimidating. Change requires being willing to move beyond our comfort zone. Transformation also necessitates a willingness to discipline our mind, which doesn't fit with the capabilities and desires of some people.

Long-distance runners are a good example of people who make positive transformations in their lives through taking small steps towards their goals. Such athletes show us the best way to reach our goals is to be content to move step-by-step towards our own finish line. We can overwhelm ourselves if we concentrate only on the huge end prize. Every long-distance runner must discipline herself to work through the pain and exhaustion of the moment. The runner may run, or walk, to the goal. Finishing the race her way, in her own time, is the object of the race.

The real reward is the discipline that's learned during the long journey of training for a race. Some people train sixteen weeks for running a marathon. What the athlete has achieved by the time she has completed the race--in her own time and in her own way—follows: energy, endurance, improved health, a deceleration of the aging process, and a positive retraining of the mind. Such achievements can eventually lead to amazing accomplishments.

We can train our minds and bodies for victory in the same way we can train them for defeat.

Overcome Our Disadvantaged Background

SOME PEOPLE PERSEVERE NO matter how many setbacks they run into on the way to the top, whatever "the top" is for them. This dedication is what gives them the edge to be successful in the end. **Success doesn't happen overnight.**

In fact, we'll find that when achievement seems to have happened quickly for certain people, those individuals have actually spent years perfecting their craft.

Often, the only difference between success and failure is the refusal to quit. Achievement can only begin when we refuse to listen to the negative voices that have taken up residence in our heads. These pessimistic voices will be happy to point out scientific facts that seem to "prove" the life that we envision for ourselves isn't possible. However, each of us is capable of believing in ourselves and accomplishing what nobody else believes can be done.

No matter what society may say, or our own self-judgment, every person has the innate capacity to improve themselves. Anyone can overcome tremendous odds as long as they are willing to move forward one step at a time. Because I refused to quit I was able to accomplish my lifelong goal of becoming an author. This book is absolute proof that anyone can overcome a deprived background.

We must usually start our own fight against low expectations. We must lead our own battle to victory. The great achievers I mentioned earlier all had to fight against low expectations and, in many cases, bullying.

However, I think it's safe to say that aggressors are not interested in improving themselves. They are only interested in tearing down people whom they perceive as weak. They may be incapable of defining improvement in any terms other than belittling other individuals. Aggressors may think that hammering someone else's ego is the only way to make them (the bullies) look stronger in the long term. This is a delusion. It goes against science.

For example, let's look at geology: Limestone and sandstone are both strong materials. They are types of rocks that can be found over much of the surface of the Earth. Granite is an even stronger type of rock, a metamorphic rock, which can be found in many places.

However, any of these rocks can be breached by an oil drill with a diamond bit because diamonds are the strongest mineral on Earth. A diamond-bit drill can breech even the strongest stone in order to allow oil to gush out of the Earth.

A bully may seem as strong as stone. Yet, even aggressors have feet of clay that can't withstand a diamond-bit drill, just like sedimentary rocks. The self-starters mentioned above probably fall into the category of "diamonds", people who surpass the level of their bullies.

Often, aggressors can find themselves unprepared to take on the real world. While they have been concentrating solely on attacking other people, critical opportunities for advances may have passed them by. Bullies may not be able to see beyond a high-school education, or a long life in their small hometown.

Unlike aggressors, devalued people may be pushed to move beyond their scarred past. They may be willing to work hard enough to make it to Hollywood, Wall Street, or whatever place they associate with success. Aggressors may not be remembered much beyond their high-school years. If they do flourish beyond high school, they may not be well known outside of their place of business.

Belligerents may not have had to work hard for anything in their lives, so they may have a complacent attitude. They may not be willing to push themselves into success. On the other hand, victims may be used to struggling on many levels. People who have pushed against judgment may find themselves fighting the life of mediocrity for which many people settle. In this way, they may catapult themselves into success. That is good news for the many undervalued individuals out there! The bullies may win the battle, but they rarely win the war! History bears out this fact.

- **Diamonds** - These gems start out as soft carbon. That carbon is, eventually, formed into one of the most valuable minerals on Earth. The process of transforming carbon-based material into diamonds is painstaking. Over millions of years, unimaginable heat and pressure compresses the carbon and drives it deeper and deeper into the Earth. By the time the diamonds are fully formed, they can only be found miles under the Earth's surface.

  Would you rather be carbon, or a diamond? Are you willing to take on the pressure of becoming a diamond? If you want to be a diamond, the strongest mineral known to man, are you going to worry about the seemingly strong limestone and granite that you will eventually be able to bore your way through?

- **Fine Porcelain** - The process of making a shapeless lump of clay into a beautiful, finished piece of priceless china is painstaking. The clay must be spun on the potter's wheel and shaped by hand. Then, the formed product must be fired in a kiln multiple times. The final steps of the process include painting and glazing.

Would you rather be a formless blob, or a priceless teacup? If you want to be a top-of-the-line piece of china, are you going to consider yourself to be in competition with the generic-brand teacups at the nearest big-box store? How would that even make sense? Priceless china (victims) is not in competition with mass-produced, big-box store, generic home goods (bullies). They aren't in the same league. That's like comparing the legendary Cal Ripken, Jr., to a minor leaguer!

The more successful we choose to be, the more complicated the process of being refined becomes. That process may include disrespect.

- **Michelangelo -** was one of the foremost artists and sculptors of the Italian Renaissance. His sculptures started out as huge slabs of the finest marble in Italy, marble from the quarry in Cararra. However, only Michelangelo could envision the masterpieces waiting to be revealed through his masterful hands. It is only through such unparalleled vision and talent that the world has been graced with works of genius such as the iconic statue of the biblical figure of David still standing in Michelangelo's hometown of Florence, Italy.

  Here is a fact that further highlights his genius: Michelangelo was only 26 years old when he won the contract to sculpt the work of art out of a slab of marble that had been in storage for decades.

  Given a choice between remaining an aging block of marble or allowing yourself to be painstakingly molded into a priceless work of art, which would you choose? Don't you want anything superfluous removed from your life, no matter how much temporary trauma that involves?

- **Tenderized Meat -** Citric acid, such as that in pineapple juice, can tenderize chicken over a period of time. A certain recipe called for two uncooked chicken breasts to be cut up into small pieces, mixed with one cup of undiluted pineapple juice, and stored in a container in a refrigerator for at least two hours.

Once I tasted chicken cooked according to the directions above, I realized I had never tasted such tender, delicious chicken outside of an upscale family restaurant.

Would you rather be fast-food chicken or upscale family-restaurant chicken?

Chapter 3

Excuses That Aggressors Use

LET ME BEGIN THIS section with an important disclaimer: I am not attempting to advocate that readers decline to accept appropriate remedies from those in authority over them. At times we may say and do certain things that need to be fixed in some way. After all, we're only human. I am only saying that we do not need to accept indiscriminate, wholesale condemnation of our character from anyone.

Correction of specific self-sabotaging behaviors is acceptable in some cases; the complete slaughter of a person's self-image is not. There is a difference. The distinction may be manifest in merely a few hastily spoken, malicious words. For instance, let's say I am the parent of a young child. This boy is struggling with his math homework. If I call my son "dumb", or say that he can't do anything right, that's a total slaughter of his character.

Those hurtful words will probably be burned in my son's psyche for a long time. On the other hand, I can choose to calmly point out, and help him to correct, specific mistakes. He probably won't feel attacked. My son will be more likely to accept my help, too.

The reality show, *America's Got Talent*, is a prime example of how people are more willing to accept constructive criticism if it is confined to specific behaviors. I have noticed that recipients of criticism on the show come in two categories:

- Some performers are likely to smile, thank the judges for their advice, and incorporate the judges' advice into their next performance. These are the performers to whom the judges give respectful, specific suggestions for improvement sandwiched in between positive comments.

- Other entertainers get defensive and combative. These are the contestants whose talent, looks, or personality, get criticized by the judges. They are given only general criticism. They are given no specific suggestions for improvement. Also, these performing artists are given no positive feedback by the judges. They feel attacked and often fight back.

Most people are willing to accept constructive criticism if it is focused solely on present concerns. On the other hand, most individuals don't want to accept criticism if it seems to aggressively attack their character. Nobody enjoys being confronted.

A second important disclaimer for this section is this: I will be relating various stories of dysfunction in my life and the lives of certain individuals. The purpose of these stories is to garner a sense of commonality in the reader. Please use these stories as a springboard to identifying, and evaluating, situations in which you felt similarly devalued. My stories are meant to be generic examples of the injustices many of us face daily.

What I Have Learned

Aggressors will always have plenty of excuses for victimizing people:

- Poor childhood training
- Not accepting the victim's religious beliefs
- Mental, or medical, challenges
- Not accepting a person's physical appearance;
- Desire for revenge for not following a bully's agenda;
- Exercising power and privilege
- Desire for high standards on the job
- Desire to pressure the victim to live up to the group mentality

It's important to note that I am at a much happier place in my life than I have ever been. Please use my narratives to build hope that we can make it through whatever struggles we have. My stories are meant to empower all the hard-working, caring, law-abiding individuals who have been disrespected for circumstances beyond their comprehension and control.

Hopefully, my stories will also serve as catalysts to more empathetic, productive behavior between the reader and the people with whom she interacts.

Every person needs to understand that we are not responsible for other peoples' negativity. We all need to question the right of certain people to treat us as inferior.

- **Anna -** She's a lady who was mentioned in the local news. She felt her time was too important to wait for school buses. Most people are aware it's the law to wait behind a school bus while it is loading and unloading children. This particular lady made a habit of driving on the sidewalk while students were boarding the bus. Finally, a parent shot video of the woman and showed it to the local police department. Anna was arrested and prosecuted.

- **Me -** I often drive my daughter to school. Parents are always in a rush to get their kids to school on time, so they can get to work. Drivers get impatient. Recently, the lady driving the car directly behind me seemed to think her time was more important than anyone else's time. She held the car horn down for about four minutes when she felt the line of cars exiting the school wasn't moving fast enough. She also honked twice at me, specifically, and pointed her finger aggressively at me. I feared a road-rage incident.

I wonder what this impatient attitude was teaching her middle-school aged child, who was sitting in the front passenger seat. Kids learn more from what we do than from what we say.

Poor Childhood Training

- **Me -** I accepted negativity from my parents as I was growing up. Please don't misunderstand; I am grateful my parents gave me the gift of life. Yet, like all of us, my parents weren't perfect. All of us have our own private hurts. My mother and father had mental and medical challenges. However, they did provide for me. My father was an intelligent man and a hard worker. Because of his self-discipline, I led a financially comfortable life in my younger years.

- **David -** is a friend whose father passed down the abuse he received from his own father because that's all he knew. This friend of mine has worked hard to be patient and kind to his own family. His kids find him to be a fun, loving father. He has broken the cycle of abuse. David is working on getting rid of the trash from his dump of a childhood.

- **Maria -** is a celebrity who is married to Greg, another celebrity. They grew up in different environments. Greg grew up in a loving home. His mother was a patient, nurturing woman who left her kids a legacy of faith, fun, love, and serenity. To this day, he remains easy-going and pleasant. On the other hand, Maria was raised in a chaotic, angry, abusive household. She had never seen fun, or peace, demonstrated. The outcome of her ridiculously dysfunctional childhood was fear and an obsessive need to control through anger. It has taken her decades to fully move from a place of bitterness and anger into a place of faith and serenity.

- **Tanya -** is a young lady I knew in my college years. She came from a family in which explosive anger was a way of life. It was standard operating procedure in Tanya's childhood home to scowl, scream, use foul language, and slam doors continually. So, what did this friend do when she got to college? She flew into rages at the slightest provocation. Luckily, this determined young lady broke the cycle of anger. She came to realize her behavior was sabotaging important relationships, so she changed her behavior. She stopped passing on the trash from her childhood.

- **Angelique**--is another lady I knew as a young adult. She honored me by giving me a simple, specific duty at her wedding reception. Her A-type mother, Cindy, had coordinated the whole reception. I had never met Cindy before. She didn't know me. Yet, the moment that I arrived at the wedding reception, she started yelling, complaining, and giving me orders. I didn't appreciate her screaming. Also, I didn't like the fact that she had given Angelique no voice in her own reception. So, I didn't follow her commands. It didn't surprise me to learn later that Cindy had always suffered from a chemical imbalance. She had made Angelique's young life miserable.

Angelique required decades to overcome the trauma from her childhood.

Not Accepting the Victim's Religious Beliefs

As I mentioned earlier, I am a member of a marginalized Christian denomination. I have been associated with this church my whole life, so I know the truth about it. For example, we worship only God. Also, we teach our members to live by the universal "Golden Rule", which states that everyone should treat others the way they want to be treated. Participants are taught to respect themselves, God, other people, and the law. However, many people do not want to hear about my value system. Numerous people want to believe the lies that can be perpetrated by certain sources of information.

It's common knowledge we can't believe everything we read and hear these days. Many news outlets follow their own agendas. Some media organizations and public figures don't concern themselves with the accuracy of their information. That is the case with most "evidence" about my church.

- **Elementary School** - I attended elementary school in a wealthy suburb in the western United States where some people consider it their right to judge other people. In my case, some people judged me as inferior because of my faith. I remember receiving two or three Valentine's Day cards out of a class of about 20 kids in my fifth-grade class. One or two of those cards were malevolent.

- **Elementary School -** That same year, I was participating in a fifth-grade spelling bee. I was one of the first students to be assigned a word. I spelled my assigned word correctly, however the teacher eliminated me from the spelling bee immediately. She admitted, with a smile, she had rejected me because she didn't like my church.

- **Junior High School -** I accidentally dropped my hairbrush while I was waiting outside in the bus lines at dismissal time. Many students saw me drop it and knew it was my hairbrush. An assistant principal picked it up off the ground and laughingly refused to give it back to me. He was well aware I missed my bus because of his refusal to return my brush. I had told him which bus was mine.

  I had to walk home. It was a long journey home, and I really didn't know the way. I had to ask a friend to point me in the right direction.

- **High School -** I went to high school in the Midwestern United States, which is known as "The Bible Belt". The dominant religion was Baptist. Therefore, my religion was not popular. I recall that one well-liked girl, Sienna, invited everyone in our history class to her birthday party except me and a Jewish girl. When questioned, Sienna admitted she hadn't invited us because she didn't like our religions.

- **High School -** On my last day of high school, I recall that two high-school staff members, who were strangers to me, disrespected me. They scowled deeply at me and, in raised voices, told me they were happy that I wasn't going to attend that school anymore; they didn't like my religion.

  One of the guidance counselors was walking by and overheard the conversation. With a frown, she reminded them they shouldn't talk to anybody like that. They didn't apologize to either me or the guidance counselor. They said they didn't care what anyone thought of their outburst; they resented my church.

- ***The Artful Detective*** - It's a show on the Ovation channel that chronicles the crime-solving skills of Detective William Murdoch in Toronto, Canada, near the end of the 19th century. In one episode, Murdock is being considered for promotion to station house inspector. In other words, he would be in full charge of everything and everybody in the station house (police precinct). When the chief inspector of Toronto police learns Murdoch is Catholic, in a predominantly Protestant city, he rejects Murdoch's application for the position.

Mental, or Medical, Challenges

SOME AGGRESSORS AND VICTIMS may be dealing with untreated medical and mental concerns. For this reason, certain individuals may be dealing with circumstances beyond their control. These people may not always be responsible for their behavior. We should always keep this in mind as we're tempted to judge them:

- **Clarissa** - was not diagnosed with depression until later in life. As a result, she raised her children in an atmosphere of negativity and anger. Yelling, criticism, and even physical abuse were common in the household. There was no feeling of acceptance or love. Her children have been striving for decades to overcome negative training with varying degrees of success.

- **Marvin** - wasn't diagnosed as being brain damaged by multiple mini-strokes until his later years. When his wife decided to move him permanently into a skilled extended-care facility, various medical testing was finally done. I'm not sure if a specific diagnosis was given. It was merely determined that his brain didn't function like other peoples' brains did. The testing finally elucidated decades of child abuse, childlike behavior, social awkwardness, negativity, and intermittent anger.

- **Karl** - was mentally ill, as we found out later. He didn't receive any treatment, or medication. He didn't admit to being abnormal. Therefore, Karl's selfishness, childishness, cruelty, and malevolence were unbounded. He routinely started rumors, based on lies, about anybody who didn't help him further his agenda. The repercussions of these lies were enormous. Business and personal relationships were ruined.

Fortunately, Karl did see consequences for his unkind actions. His girlfriend left him, he lost his job, and he was sent back to his country of origin.

Not Accepting a Person's Physical Appearance

UNITED STATES SOCIETY IS obsessed with appearance. We may judge people by any number of characteristics related to the way they look and dress. We're likely to appraise a person based on whether their overall appearance is generally pleasing to us. In a nutshell, we tend to judge any aspect of an individual's appearance that places them outside of our own social circle.

I know many average people who have been disrespected because, through no fault of their own, their appearance kept them on the fringes of popular groups. I'm certain the reader will be able to think of many examples from his own life.

Revenge for Not Following an Aggressor's Agenda

CONTROLLING PEOPLE DO NOT like to be manipulated, or to have their agendas obstructed. At one company, I was responsible for persuading the owner to cut some of the inappropriate privileges of Sandy. She was a worker who felt a sense of entitlement. Sandy felt I had disrupted her plans. She took her revenge by spreading malicious lies about me to anyone that would listen. The untruths resulted in broken business and personal relationships.

Desire for Power and Privilege

SOME PEOPLE FEEL THAT being in a position of power and privilege entitles them to treat other people with disdain. It's a well-known fact that some politicians, celebrities, and law enforcement officers don't care how they treat people they consider to be inferior to them. There are a myriad of stories regarding how some celebrities disrespect fans, members of the press, employees, individuals with less celebrity status than them, and even blood relatives. It's no secret politicians may disrespect other politicians and constituents who don't agree with their value system and agenda.

James was stopped for speeding on a narrow, two-lane country road. Since he felt it was unsafe to stop in the exact spot indicated by the motorcycle officer, he slowly drove his car a few feet ahead. The officer stopped his motorcycle in front of James' car, dismounted, and held his hand out aggressively in a "stop" position. Then, the officer yelled, "Did I tell you to stop here? You stop where I tell you to!" He continued to demean my friend for the next few minutes.

Other groups of people who may feel they have a right to abuse their position of authority include teachers, parents, and bosses. Some educators may feel that they have no need to be respectful and helpful to students.

Examples of parents who abuse their head-of-the-household authority are too numerous to list here. There are also many examples of bosses who abuse their authority by being discourteous, overloading employees with unexpected assignments, and ignoring the personal needs of their employees.

What I Have Learned

I HAVE DISCOVERED NUMEROUS reasons that some people become aggressors:

- **Immaturity--**Some people haven't moved beyond childish behavior. The triggers for the people who bullied me involved my not acting the way they wanted me to act, or believing what they wanted me to believe. Now, I realize only an immature, insecure, person would think it's a good idea if everyone is forced to look and act like he does. A well-adjusted person knows diversity can only enrich any given society.

   Most people realize that a conformist environment where everyone acts the same is non-existent. To use a musical analogy: both harmony and melody are necessary to produce full-bodied music. If we play the melody alone, the song might seem two-dimensional and flat. If we play the harmony alone, the song will seem confusing and unfinished. However, if we combine both the harmony and the melody, we will get the rich, three-dimensional sensory experience intended by the composer. Every part of the puzzle will fit together nicely.

- **A feeling of superiority--**Self-righteousness can be loosely defined as the attitude of a person who feels he is superior to people who don't think, look, act, talk, or believe as he does. The harasser might also scorn people who don't make as much money as he does. Quite often, the arrogant person may be openly abusive and scornful. History (and current events) is full of examples of sanctimonious people who trample on the freedom, civil rights, and dignity of people who they consider to be inferior.

- **A wrong mindset--**Aggressors may have been traumatized in their youth. Also, they may be dealing with current psychological and physical challenges. The bully may have incomplete knowledge about certain groups as well. All of these situations can lead to inaccurate thinking.

- **Insecurity--**It's a well-known sports-related saying that the best defense is offense. If you think about it, no defense should be needed for an entity that is completely secure in every way. (For example, we often hear of people robbing convenience stores. On the other hand, how many people try to break into Fort Knox, where America's gold is stored?) For many people, the easiest way to defend an insecure personality is to go on the offensive. This leads to the conclusion that a major motivation of bullying may be insecurity.

- **Selfishness**--Certain individuals only care about furthering their own plans. These people often choose to follow their agendas with selfishness and cruelty. This is manifest in many forms of unprofessional and unethical conduct, including the abuse of power and privilege.

Desire for High Standards on the Job

WHO HASN'T EXPERIENCED TRASH talk on the job? I'm sure most people, if they were honest, would say they have heard, participated in, or been the victim of disrespectful speech on the job:

- **Temporary Employment -** I accepted a one-day job through a temporary employment agency. The job was an entry-level position at a major grocery-store chain. I was responsible for cleaning and stocking the bakery of the supermarket. My supervisor felt no need to be courteous to me, or to explain my duties to me in an easily comprehensible manner. She also gave me physically arduous duties to which I was not supposed to be assigned. As a consequence, I got sluggish, and my back started hurting. When I get tired, and my body starts hurting, I don't always listen well. I don't think well, either. My brain seems to slow down, even shut down, as well as my body. By the end of my shift, the supervisor was yelling at me and calling me "Stupid."

- **Student Teaching -** I almost became a secondary education teacher. I even rose to the level of student teacher at a high school. (Student teaching is the final step education students take before graduation. It is seven to eight weeks of hands-on training in a classroom.) There is no general handbook for teachers. Non-specific college classes and on-the-job training is all there is. However, I found that my supervising teacher, Betsy, expected me to be fully trained in the complicated job of teaching. She expected me to be prepared to step into a full-time teaching position immediately. Betsy gave me no positive feedback. She expected me to plan lessons, teach a creative writing class, do administrative work, and do word processing on a computer with no training in any of these areas. Betsy gave me no help, but she was always quick to criticize my efforts to me and my supervisors. The more she censored me, the slower and less confident I became. I declined to graduate with a teaching certification attached to my degree.

- **Bank Teller** - Numbers have never been my strong point, and I was a slow learner. The more mistakes I made, the more my supervisor, Amber, yelled at me. The screaming made me confused and slow, so I made even more errors. It was a vicious cycle. I stopped initiating any conversation with Amber. Who wants to ask questions of a person who only raises their voice? I got fired because I was "too slow".

- **Publishing** - The second paid job from which I got fired was a copy editing/proofreading job in a small office. Copy eciting and proofreading are complicated jobs. Nevertheless, I was a competent worker in the beginning. Eventually, my supervisor noticed I was not catching on to certain duties as quickly as I should. She complained. She made no secret of letting me know my work was not satisfactory. The more she complained, the slower I became.

What I Have Learned

Some people with whom we interact may not have our best interests at heart.

IF WE DO HAPPEN to be grouped with kind, nurturing bosses and coworkers, we can consider that a blessing. Many people are going to fall in line with human nature, which means many people will be more concerned with their own agendas than with others' goals. In addition, people might not be willing, or able, to meet all of our needs and expectations.

Everyone Operates at Different Capacities.

What is easy for some people is difficult for other people. For example, as a substitute teacher, I notice that some students may require a detailed explanation of certain concepts while other students may not.

In my case, I needed patience from my supervisors, which some of them were unwilling and unable to give. They felt I didn't learn certain crucial concepts as quickly as I could. However, in my mind, I was learning as fast as I could.

- **My Kids -** When both of my children were younger, I enrolled them in an outdoor soccer league for three seasons. I thought it was important to get them involved in sports. However, they were both miserable. Athletics didn't come as easily to them as it does to some other kids. They tried their best, but neither of them performed as well as they had hoped. They tired easily, got minor injuries, and got exposed to extremes in weather. The worst part was that they compared themselves, unfavorably, to the other team members. Some of the other team members were gifted in soccer.

  I finally accepted the fact that neither of my kids had a passion for serious soccer. Wisely, I stopped enrolling my kids in leagues. I have come to peace with their true strengths: music, electronics, and academics.

- **George and Janet--**They are both over eighty years old. She is reaping the harvest of a lifetime of wise lifestyle choices. Janet is active. She walks almost every day. She eats plenty of fresh food. She works almost full time. She drives, cooks, does her own shopping, and cleans and repairs her own condominium. She has only a few minor health concerns. On the other hand, George is reaping a harvest of a lifetime of unwise lifestyle choices. He has many ongoing major medical problems. He has always been sedentary and overindulged in unhealthy food. He is in and out of the hospital often. He has had a myriad of major medical concerns since young adulthood.

Obviously, George has less physical strength than Janet. This is a fact that must be accepted. Yelling at the man, expecting him to do more, would produce no positive results. It would be counterproductive, cruel, and ludicrous. It is beyond his capacity to be as productive as Janet.

- **Cedric--**He's been a sports and outdoors enthusiast for his whole life. He has expected his family to follow his lead, as well. For decades, he and his active family have participated in almost every sport. When this man coordinates family reunions, the activities center solely on outdoor sports like skiing and white-water rafting. That isn't good news for family members who are elderly, unfit, have debilitating medical conditions, or are uninterested in sports. Obviously, my friend thinks only of his own desires when he plans family reunions. He doesn't take into consideration varying ages, interests, or aptitudes.

We must all accept the fact that everyone has different capabilities, and that's what makes the world go around.

No amount of yelling is going to turn the Helen Kellers into Navy fighter pilots, or the Einsteins into sports prodigies. We are what we are, and we should embrace that fact. Each of us is capable of contributing, in our own way, to the society in which we live. Any society would be diminished without people who are able to contribute a wide variety of interests, knowledge, and skills. Nobody should be sidelined because they don't appear to have all the most sought-after skills. (For that matter, who has the right to determine what the most sought-after skills should be?) The bottom line is that one never knows what a person has to offer, if that person is given the freedom to live in line with their own truth and capabilities.

The victim is often pressured to follow the accepted group's mentality.

- **My College Years -** I left home at the age of 17 to go to college for the first time. The school that I chose was a private, conservative university. The employees and students were expected to excel in their studies, their work, and their treatment of other people. The sponsor of the university was known for shaping hard-working, socially-conscious people. I was hoping that I would feel accepted at this university. However, some of the people who I chose to befriend didn't follow the school's attitude of tolerance. Their group belittled certain individuals, including myself. That was hard for a naïve 17-year-old to take. The fact that my "friends" involved their accepted group in demeaning language was even harder to take. I found that strangers were spreading rumors about me, and mere acquaintances were yelling at me. It was clear I was being judged as inferior by the group.

- ***13 Going on 30* -** This movie is a recent illustration of stories about marginalized people who try to fit into popular groups only to find that popular groups leave a person feeling unfulfilled. The film was made in 2004, and it stars Jennifer Garner. Her character, Jenna, begins in the movie as a 13-year old who gets taken advantage of by the cool students because she wants to fit in with them. Jenna even joins them in devaluing the sterling character of a boy she has known for years, Matt.

Magic dust on Matt's birthday gift to Jenna helps her to fulfill her wish of becoming a 30-year-old woman. She finds that her 30-year-old self has made a mess of her life. She finally realizes the popular crowd was not worth her time.

She senses that the humble Matt, now a struggling photographer, was the main person worth loving and respecting all along. After Jenna goes back in time (to her 13th year) to straighten out her life, she and Matt get married. Also, she severs ties with the leader of the cool crowd.

- ***Dear Bully: 70 Authors Tell Their Stories* –** I highly recommend this book. It is an anthology of 70 well-known Young Adult fiction authors' reminiscences regarding bullying during their younger years. The tales are heartfelt first-hand accounts of being victims, perpetrators, and witnesses of diminishing conflicts. Some stories are amusing and some are sad. However, all of the accounts left me wondering why any of us work so hard to fit into cliques that demean people for unfair reasons in a juvenile manner.

Most accounts deal with aggressors dehumanizing young people because they don't look and act a certain way, or befriend only popular groups or people. Every story highlighted the idea that bullies may use the slightest excuse to exclude victims from the "most admired" relationships. **If we must devalue ourselves in order to pursue a relationship of any kind, we might want to ask ourselves if the connection is worth our time and effort.**

WE DON'T NEED TO be members of the popular groups if these cliques don't treat individuals with respect. Sometimes, the price of being popular is too high. It may go against our inner voice. Conscience is the inner truth within us that tells us what's right and what's wrong. It's universal across most cultures and faiths. Most people care about treating themselves, and other people, with respect. Why should we want to be part of a group that belittles other people, when we know that's not right?

Traditionally, in movies and T.V., there are powerful groups that don't treat people right. There are also undervalued groups that do treat people right. Many Disney movies come to mind as do many fairy tales. The plot line is cut and dried. The good guys always win. *Snow White and the Seven Dwarfs*, and *Cinderella*, are both classic examples of this archetype. Snow White and Cinderella, the undervalued stars, both get their prince and their kingdom in the end. The selfish villains in classic fairy tales usually get disenfranchised in some way.

The lines between good and evil may seem to be uncertain in Hollywood lately. Yet, most of us are still aware of the efficacy of treating people with the respect all humans crave.

It makes sense to crave membership in low-maintenance, low-profile groups rather than popular groups. **It might not be prudent to strive for acceptance in a clique that will demand we sacrifice our individualism and self-respect**. We should seek to interact with people who are committed to treating everyone with dignity.

The Final Word on Trash Talk from Others

PEOPLE ARE PRONE TO demean and fear what they do not fully understand. Along with that, people reserve the right to decide what sources of information they deem credible. In summary, people will believe what they want to believe.

- **The Druids** - were a secretive society of pagan Celtic priests, mainly centered in parts of what is now the United Kingdom around the 1st Century AD. They kept no written records. Few facts remain about their beliefs and practices. The Roman emperor, Julius Caesar, ruled over most of the known world at that time, including the United Kingdom. He capitalized on the fact that little was known about the Druids by building up a fear of them. Perhaps he did this because he wanted his people, especially his soldiers, to feel they had the right to continue to repress the Celtic people. Apparently, Caesar told his people many stories about how the Druids tortured and killed people. We may never know how many of his stories were true. Yet, history records his people believed the stories. Roman soldiers did kill Druids.

- **The Japanese**--After WWII, hundreds of Japanese civilians refused to come out of a certain cave where they had been hiding from Allied forces for an extended period of time. This was because their own countrymen had terrified them with propaganda of how the Americans would mistreat them, even kill them. The exiles were aware the war was over, but they chose to remain in the cave out of fear. They refused to believe their former enemy would allow them to calmly exit the cave and return to whatever normal life they could make for themselves. American soldiers had to go into the cave to escort the sickly, starving people to safety. The refugees, finally, realized they had been told lies about the former enemies of their country.

The Positive Side

The upside to my failed jobs is that I was divinely guided not to keep any of those jobs. The doors that had initially opened to provide me these jobs were closed for a reason. In each case, I was brought to a new level of life. I was led to important new relationships, better job opportunities, and the chance to get out of debt.

Like many people, I have plenty of other examples of jobs for which I interviewed, but didn't get the position.

If I had become successful in any of those careers, I would have been stuck in unappealing, low-paying spots that I would have eventually been forced to give up because of health concerns, or other life changes. That would have been more embarrassing than not getting the job in the first place!

Closed doors always provide a divine opportunity to be led to more fulfilling, gratifying open doors. It's a clear case of hindsight being 20-20. The loss of each job mentioned earlier led to my marriage and enhanced career opportunities.

Sometimes, we must be patient. At first, newly-opened doors may not always look like fresh opportunities. Prospects may not always manifest themselves immediately. In fact, opportunities may first present themselves as unexpected, undesired challenges. The good news is those trials are what prepare us for new levels in life.

Chapter 4

The Power of Positive Feedback

IN RETROSPECT, I HAVE decided I was worthy of having more confidence during the traumatic times detailed above. I was doing the best I could with limited resources. I just wasn't catching on to some of my work duties as quickly as expected.

I should have asked for clarification of my duties before the drama escalated to the point that my bosses felt they absolutely could no longer work with me. It's possible my supervisors may have been happy to simplify my duties. After all, they had an investment in keeping their companies running smoothly.

According to my bosses, I was a liability because I was mentally slow and had an attitude. To my way of thinking, my mind was on overload. I had no desire, or ability, to process all that was thrown at me in an angry manner.

The Importance of Words

AS ANY MOTIVATIONAL SPEAKER can attest, words are full of power. One word can be just as powerful as a one-hour speech. The proof of this is in the immediate emotional reaction of a person who hears a word like "stupid", or "smart". To expand the example: consider the effect of an extended period of positive or negative communication. I could cite multiple examples of people I know who carry scars from being exposed to years of negativity, especially during their childhoods. I could also cite examples of well-adjusted people who have never been exposed to a vast amount of pessimism in their lives.

One example of the strength of words can be found in the speech of British Prime Minister, Winston Churchill, at the Harrow School on October 29th, 1941. This was a dark time for England. All of Britain would remember the recent Blitz. The length of the speech may vary according to the source. However, the main gist of the inspirational speech has retained its power for over six decades: we should never give up hope, or give in to the enemy's desire to crush our dreams.

Reputations can be made, or broken, on the strength of merely a few words. Whether the words are true seems to be immaterial. Many people are going to believe what they want despite evidence to the contrary. The important thing to remember is that it's human nature to believe rumors from even unreliable sources. We often don't question the credibility of the many fountains of negativity in the world as often as we should. Unreliable sources might be discredited in the end. In the meantime, the damage has already been done.

Decades ago, an American newspaper published hearsay that led to the death of a young man. Isaac, a slim, petit African-American teenager, was convicted of the double murder of two white girls with a blunt object. The evidence was only circumstantial. No witnesses were brought forth by either the defense or the prosecution. Logistically speaking, the chance of such a small boy being able to physically overcome the two girls in such a brutal way was remote.

The fact that he was one of the last people known to have seen the girls alive may have been his only link to the crime. The newspapers judged him guilty with a few words. The mayor judged him guilty based on the carelessly researched newspaper accounts. Relatives of the boy continue to maintain that his multiple confessions to an ecclesiastical leader were false, given under duress. Supporters of the boy believed he was sentenced to die without solid evidence.

We cannot physically retract unkind words. We can apologize or explain, but no more. Impassioned words may be remembered for decades, whether they are encouraging or destructive. One of the most well-known current maxims is that nobody should post anything in cyberspace that may embarrass them, or get them in trouble. Spoken words can be compared to a bag of feathers opened to the blowing wind, or to shredded paper. In both of these cases, the pieces cannot be put back together.

Jon Scieszka, a famous American young adult fiction author, describes how individuals may remember unkind words for decades through his story in the anthology I mentioned earlier, *Dear Bully: 70 Authors Tell Their Stories*. He and his friends nicknamed a fellow student "Stench" for obvious reasons. In turn, those same friends nicknamed Scieszka "Green Bean" because of a particular pair of green corduroy pants he wore.

The Folly of Criticism

CRITICISM IS NOT A foolproof way to handle adverse circumstances. Trash talk is not a permanent solution. It may only encourage the victim to believe that he is unable to rise above the level of inadequacy. If a person is constantly criticized, he may start to believe he has no ability to improve. **A person must hope that he has the capability of becoming a better person before he will put effort into improving himself.** Constant criticism is likely to kill any hope of a better life for most people.

Verbal harassment accomplishes nothing constructive. Such harassment only produces fear, or anger--and a serious mental disconnect between the abuser and the victim--in the short term. For example, the friend I mentioned earlier who was abused by his father has never had a desire to be deeply involved with his father.

There's a famous saying: you catch more flies with honey than with vinegar. If we want people at any level of society to cooperate with us, we need to treat them well. What goes around comes around, as the well-known aphorism says. Kindness is likely to pay dividends down the road in the form of unexpected favors. One example of this is found in the reality series, *Undercover Boss*. This is a show in which one of the top bosses of a large corporation works undercover among her lower-level employees in order to determine what's working and what isn't working in her company. Some of the employees who "train" the bosses in their position for the day are patient and respectful, while others aren't. The helpful trainers are rewarded at the end of the show with promotions, vacations, and money. The discourteous, unmotivated trainers are reprimanded.

People of different personalities will react in varying ways when they are confronted. Some personality types will completely retreat into their shells and shut down when they are bombarded with negativity.

An extreme example of this is a short movie called *Cipher in the Snow*. This is a true story about Chris, a young school boy who was so belittled by his stepfather and school teachers that he decided life was no longer worth living.

He got off the school bus one day, lay down in the snow, and simply died. A second personality type is likely to distance themselves from the offending person, or situation. A third personality type is likely to get defensive immediately and lash out at the slightest hint of even "constructive" criticism, uncaring of the consequences. As for the fourth category of people: it's my guess that recipients of aggressive negativity who immediately accept instruction and vow to act in a more socially acceptable manner are few. How many individuals are that humble and well-adjusted?

The varying reactions that people can have when faced with negativity is illustrated in two reality shows I watch: *Mystery Diners* and *Restaurant Stakeout*. In these shows, the bosses of restaurants pay someone to come in and film everything that happens in their restaurant for a day. The owners want their restaurants to be staked out so they can see why their business isn't performing well. Few of the troublesome employees who are confronted apologize at once, vow to work harder, and ask for a second chance. Most of the confronted employees react in one of the following predictable ways: cussing and storming out, accusing other employees, walking away before the boss finishes talking to them, begging to keep their jobs for financial reasons, or getting defensive.

In my experience, most people will want to perform in a more socially acceptable manner only if they feel accepted. Each individual must believe in their own capacity to improve. Actions are motivated by hope. All actions start as thoughts. **We cannot accomplish what we do not first envision in our minds.**

Every positive action that we take is motived by a belief that we can perform that feat. Every undesirable deed stems from the lack of hope that we are capable of acting in a more appropriate manner.

Let me rephrase those last thoughts: **If we don't receive much optimistic input in our lives, we might not believe in our ability to improve ourselves.**

The Self-Fulfilling Prophecy

A SELF-FULFILLING PROPHECY IS a particular way we analyze ourselves. For instance, I believed I was moving and thinking too slowly in certain jobs; therefore, I actually started going progressively slower.

On the other hand, I am also familiar with the positive side of self-fulfilling prophecy: there is a short film first produced decades ago, called *Johnny Lingo*. The movie is about a young Hawaiian woman named Mahana who was shunned and scorned by most of the people she knew; therefore, she believed she was of no worth. Nobody thought she would ever get married. The woman's face was emotionally dark and shadowed, and she always walked with her head hanging down. In fact, Mahana often hid in trees because she felt ostracized.

In those days, it was the tradition for the prospective groom to give the father of the bride a practical gift, usually cows. The scornful villagers couldn't imagine how any man would give this young lady's father even two cows for the "privilege" of marrying his daughter. Imagine their surprise when one of the most eligible bachelors on the island, Johnny Lingo, asked this young lady's father for her hand in marriage. He offered eight cows as his wedding gift. That was far above the amount of cows that even the most respected of the village matrons had commanded on the eve of their own weddings.

The result of this unprecedented faith in the ostracized girl was that she became a productive, confident, member of her village for the first time.

She also felt free to let her natural beauty shine forth and began acting and looking similar to an eight-cow woman. She began satisfying her husband's high expectations. She stopped achieving her detractors' low expectations.

The Value of High Expectations

IN THE SAME WAY as Mahana, I have had some success in fulfilling my own husband's high expectations. He saw potential in me that nobody before him had seen. I was his eight-cow wife, even when I seemed like a no-cow person. He has believed in me through the decades of health and career challenges. My husband did not see who I was; he saw who I could become with the help of his love. After 23 years of marriage, he is still validating me with his attitude of faith, mercy, and love. Since he believes in me, I believe in myself. Otherwise, I wouldn't be able to write this book.

Chapter 5

The Need for Respect in Relationships
(Why We Should Not Let Trash Talk Bother Us)

You are acceptable as you are.

YOU CAN BREAK THE cycle of negativity in your life. You are allowed to fight domination and negative self-talk. If you are a solid, law-abiding citizen, you are as worthy as the next person. Don't let self-righteous people pin their own homemade labels to you. Just tear their labels off and throw them away! Judgmental people can be narrow minded and cruel. They don't see your full potential, and they might not be aware of the mitigating circumstances behind your behavior. One illustration of this is found in the fact that people who have a lot of resources to devote to improving their appearance often feel it's their right to judge people who are unable to put as much emphasis on their looks.

Most people are budget conscious by necessity. For example, the other day I was served by a low-level employee at a local grocery store who was missing most of her bottom teeth. She wasn't a senior citizen. She wasn't close to the age that is most associated with denture wearers. Some people might have felt they had a right to judge this lady as lacking in appearance. Yet, if we look at it from another angle, how can we judge her for neglecting to fix what she does not have the resources to fix?

Every person works within his own framework of abilities and resources.

EVERY PERSON HAS A divine right to make his own choices regarding his behavior, his appearance, and his beliefs. Each individual will make decisions based on his physical and financial capabilities. However, every person should make sure that his choices are considered ethical, legal, and appropriate, for the society in which he lives.

We all have potential.

THERE ARE MILLIONS OF examples of people who refused to wear labels that said that they were inferior:

- **Shaquille "The Shaq" O'Neal**--is widely known as one of the most skilled basketball players of all time. He was given negative labels by his basketball coach when he was in his early teens. His coach said he was too big and slow. O'Neal got cut from the team. Yet, O'Neal refused to accept these labels as permanent. With a lot of practice and mentoring, he honed his skills to the point where he won a spot on Louisiana State University's basketball team. Since then, he has played basketball professionally. He has also accomplished guest appearances on certain TV shows as well as commercial endorsements.

- **Joel Osteen**--is head pastor of Lakewood Church in Houston, Texas. He leads what is generally regarded as the largest Protestant congregation in America. However, he had negative labels pinned on him when he first took over the ministry about fifteen years ago. He overheard some people in his congregation critically comparing him to his predecessor, his own beloved father. The fact was that Joel Osteen had no formal education, training, or experience in ministry. He ran T.V. production for Lakewood. Some of his congregation even wondered aloud if the church would survive the change in leadership. Today, Joel Osteen continues to lead his church as well as hold stadium-filled inspirational gatherings throughout the English-speaking world. He is also a prolific New York Times bestselling author.

Labels are Subjective.

SINCE UNFLATTERING LABELS MAY vary from group to group, why should we accept them? Different cultures may prize varied personality and physical characteristics. Some societies revere youth and outgoing personalities while others don't. Who has the right to say which culture is right, and which is wrong? It's all in the training. Just because our little corner of the world abides by certain social mores doesn't mean everyone else should follow them.

Throughout history, western culture has devalued some individuals because of their unique characteristics, particularly if they were short in stature:

- **James Madison**--was the Fourth President of the United States. He stood approximately 5'4" tall, weighed in at barely 111 pounds, and had medical concerns. His challenges didn't stop him from becoming the Father of the Constitution, Thomas Jefferson's Secretary of State, the supervisor of the drafting of the Louisiana Purchase, and the man who led the United States to victory in the War of 1812.

- **Napoleon Bonaparte**--was the emperor of France for ten years. He was another leader who was diminutive in stature by today's standards. Modern historians place his height at somewhere between 5'4" and 5'6". Yet, he is still widely regarded as one of the finest military minds in history. His power extended much further than his homeland, the small island of Corsica off the coast of Italy. He conquered, formed alliances with, or attempted to conquer much of the known world of his day. This includes a significant portion of land that was later sold to the government of the United States under the Louisiana Purchase.

- **Lindsey Stirling**--is a world-renown violinist and dancer who made her fame on YouTube. She is a recent example of a person who refused to accept the labels that some individuals wanted to pin on her. Her videos average over 1,000,000 views. She guests on TV talk shows and travels the world performing.

Lindsey did have to struggle to win acceptance. She composes her own music, and her music cannot be categorized as traditional classical music. Also, she is one of the first people to blend original compositions with various genres of dance. She thinks outside the box. This ability to expand the horizons of performance may not be appreciated by everyone.

Lindsey made it to the quarter finals during one season of the reality show, *America's Got Talent*. However, at least two of the judges made unkind remarks about her playing. They felt she should play more traditional music backed by a traditional musical ensemble.

Lindsey refused to accept their labels. She pulled them off and threw them away.

- **The High-Fashion Industry--**is a model (pun intended) of subjective labeling. Many females throughout the world would probably be insecure if we all believed we were obligated to follow the trends of New York, Paris, and Milan. Would it even be appropriate if women dressed in high fashion for every occasion, or spent hours on their beauty routine daily? Would we want a 20-year old Victoria's Secret™ model in our boardroom? Should we expect female farmers to feed the livestock in evening gowns and stilettos? Would male Wall Street stock brokers want to be distracted by scantily clad female co-workers?

Trash talk is not always personal.

DISRESPECTFUL CONVERSATION CAN BE the result of indolence, or selfishness. The truth is that some people can't be bothered to determine why you are acting the way you do. They just react to you in a knee-jerk response. They might not even have issues with you, personally. They may just be passing on the trauma from their own lives. Yes, there are evil people out there. Yet, most individuals act the way they do because of selfishness, poor childhood training, traumatic current environment, or medical and mental challenges.

People act out of their own pain, and we all have pain. Some people are likely to inflict their hurt on other people.

THERE ARE MANY CONDITIONS that can skew an individual's behavior. Some people have damaged emotions. That means they don't think right.

The main example that comes to my mind is from *Mystery Diners*. In a particular episode, Marvin, the chef, was shown to degrade only the male server. Also, he ignored the needs of the female servers who he considered to be unattractive. Along the same lines, he acted inappropriately friendly with some of the female servers who he considered to be attractive. At the end of that episode, viewers were informed the troubled employee was seeking professional counseling.

Disrespectful communication is often a manifestation of the self-obsession of today's society.

MORE PEOPLE SEEM TO be selfish than ever before. Common courtesy seems to be a thing of the past in many cases. Numerous people put no filter on their words merely because they can't get beyond their own problems. These kinds of people aren't going to worry about how their hasty, unkind words may affect their listeners. All they're concerned with is their own sorrow:

Jeff is a well-known motivational speaker who dealt with a distracted cashier after waiting in a long checkout line at a grocery store. He noticed the employee was consistently rude to the other customers. Despite the cashier's attitude, Jeff determined to be pleasant to her. He decided not to let her bad mood dictate his own mood. When it was his turn to pay for his groceries, the employee repeated her pattern of rudeness. However, she begged Jeff's forgiveness when she learned who he was, explained that she had just had traumatizing family news, and asked if he would pray for her. In the end, Jeff was glad he hadn't used dehumanizing communication in a knee-jerk response to the cashier's disrespectful tone of voice.

Some people don't consider how powerful words are. In truth, physical wounds can heal much quicker than psychological wounds caused by hurtful words.

Certain individuals become accustomed to language that devalues other people during their childhood; it's all they know.

IN SUCH CASES, TRASH talk might not be personal. It seems people who are exposed to mentally healthy social interactions during their younger years are the most likely people to pass down that same behavior. We often continue the conduct we see modeled during our childhood.

In this way, multiple generations can pass down abuse. I know of two families in which severe abuse was passed down through at least three generations. The reason for the abuse, according to Dan, a former abuser of his own children, was the lack of modeling of correct behavior during his own childhood. He didn't know any other way to act. Dan didn't hate his own kids; he just didn't know that his actions were wrong. He didn't know there was an alternative to raising kids in an abusive manner.

We should not be judged for that which is beyond our control.

THERE ARE PEOPLE AT the apex of every group who consider themselves to be the arbiters of worthiness in the group. I've heard it said that history is written by the victors. These days, I think it's also true that some history is being re-written by today's most powerful people. Any given society is regulated by winners. The standing of the champions may come from any combination of military, financial, political, or social power. The masses of everyday people are expected to follow the dictates of the people at the top of their social group, even though they may not always have the capacity to do so:

- A child cannot control the level of his household income, his family's behavior, or his parents' work ethic.
- A medically disadvantaged person may not be able to completely control some of his own behaviors, even with medical help.
- Some students will not perform to the same academic level as other students.
- Certain people will not have as many social skills as other people. They may be incapable of a high level of appropriate social interaction.

If you think about it, does it even make sense to judge people for something that is beyond their control?

Internalizing dehumanizing speech is unhealthy; it can cause blockage in our bodies.

TRASH TALK CAN CAUSE stress and anxiety. Medical experts agree these disruptive emotions can lead to malfunction throughout the body, including blockage. Pathology is usually caused by an obstruction of some sort. A healthy body is one in which every system works together to keep the body running like a well-oiled machine.

I would like to use an extended analogy to illustrate this point: I recently noticed my clothes dryer wasn't working efficiently. I knew I hadn't gotten my dryer vent cleaned properly in years. A company came out to clean our entire duct system, including the dryer vent. However, it took three trips to my house for the company to determine that a major blockage in the duct system was the cause of the dryer malfunction. This obstruction was in a hard-to-reach place, and had not broken completely free when the initial cleaning was done.

The technicians had to bring in heavy equipment in order to loosen the blockage, which was the size of a large bird's nest. The workers used high-pressure air to loosen the obstruction and free it from the system of ducts. The blockage, the hidden "disease", had built up over the fifteen-year life span of our house.

The impediment didn't happen overnight. Over a decade of stress had built up in our ducts. Blockage in a vent system is a major fire hazard just as any sort of obstacle in our mind and body is a health hazard.

The perils of obstructions in our bodies are abundant. In my limited experience, people who work to keep stress out of their lives don't usually have severe problems with their gastrointestinal tract. As a consequence, such people often don't look their chronological age. On the other hand, I know quite a few people who seem to live in crisis mode. These individuals often look older than their years. They also seem to be constantly dealing with major medical problems of some sort. We all have our trials to deal with; that's life. Our reactions to these trials will be a determining factor in our health.

We don't need to allow ourselves to get sick over the unfairness of life because bullies are likely to pay a price for their cruelty in the end.

IT'S AN IMMUTABLE LAW of the universe: what goes around comes around. A gardener might call it **"The Law of the Harvest."** You reap what you sew. If you plant only tomatoes, you cannot expect to harvest carrots. In the same way, if people "plant" only pessimism, they will "harvest" only pessimism at some point.

It may manifest itself in personal, or medical, challenges. In the meantime, if we internalize their disapproval, we may be the only ones who immediately suffer.

In a sort of divine retribution, some abusers reap an immediate harvest. I live in a densely populated area of the United States. Because of this, I see constant examples of road rage. For example, Jared made the local headlines when he was driving his truck one day. He honked, yelled, and made an obscene gesture as he zoomed recklessly around a slower, smaller vehicle in his lane. Jared's harvest was to immediately crash into the ditch in the middle of the road. He not only crashed, his whole truck came apart. Automotive parts went flying out of his engine and scattered everywhere. A serious car wreck was his yield from a crop of road rage.

We can make our own choices, but we cannot choose the consequences of those choices.

POOR CHOICES REAP POOR harvests. Those yields may manifest themselves in a number of ways. For example, stress can affect many systems of the body. That's a truth that relates to both the abuser and the victim. In some cases, harassed people may be able to let the universe right its own wrongs in order to keep sane and healthy. Some wrongs may right themselves if we mentally distance ourselves and allow them to naturally resolve themselves. We must pick and choose that on which we expend our precious emotional energy.

You may not be responsible for medical issues that limit your own abilities.

AS I STATED EARLIER, I am gluten intolerant. Eating gluten for decades affected every part of my body, including my brain; I ignored various pathological medical, and psychological, symptoms.

I didn't know that my diverse symptoms could be labeled as medically unusual. I just thought it was my fate to be dissimilar from other people. When my symptoms first started manifesting, gluten intolerance wasn't widely discussed. I wouldn't have suspected that an integral part of my diet was slowly sabotaging my health, my relationships, my jobs, and my education.

Clara is the wife of a local ecclesiastical leader who was recently diagnosed with aggressive cancer. This lady is a young, energetic mother of five young children. She has been a healthy, hard-working woman. Clara has had no difficulties being a full-time mom, keeping her household organized, and serving in her church. However, it's not surprising that her energy has gone downhill since she started various treatments for cancer.

Right now, Clara does not have the capability to accomplish everything she used to do. She is working within a new "normal". For example, she is, generally, a friendly, gregarious person. Yet, she has asked that people do not visit her house, or bring food right now. Also, she hasn't attended church in about two months. Therefore, her fellow church members have stepped up and offered to help in many different areas. After all, young children cannot be left to their own devices. Houses don't clean themselves. Food doesn't cook itself. Households don't manage themselves, either.

Medical concerns can cause the sufferer to be deceived in their thinking.

I KNOW PEOPLE WHO have a hard time seeing anything in a positive light. These are individuals who will interpret everything people say and do in an unflattering manner. Also, they may imagine only worst-case scenarios. For example, I play the piano for the kids' church organization in my church. I make mistakes, as most people would. I blow my mistakes out of proportion. I am always sure everyone heard my mistakes, and they consider my piano playing to be inferior. I even go so far as to worry that one of the kids' church leaders will ask me to vacate my position due to my ineptitude.

The actual feedback I get tells me that I'm a skilled piano player. Some of the parents have followed my piano playing for years; they say that I am becoming a more proficient player. So, do I believe my own way of thinking, which I admit is often stuck in a negative groove? Or, do I believe the positive feedback?

Some people are deceived in their evaluation of social situations:

- **Caroline--**seems to have mental challenges. I don't know if she's gluten intolerant because she hasn't been tested. However, it's my belief something has compromised the clarity of her thinking. The main indicator of this is the fact that she has always felt she's incredibly attractive to the opposite sex. Her looks might be categorized as average. Yet, she imagines some men find her overwhelmingly beautiful and some women are jealous of her. To my mind, this lady's thinking is cloudy in at least one area.

- **Janet--**has Asperger's Syndrome, a high-functioning form of autism. She got mainstreamed as a student, but she was socially awkward. She didn't always interact in a healthy manner with other people. She has even been known to be inappropriately aggressive. Jane has offended some people because of her inability to express herself in a suitable manner. Even as an adult, Janet is uncomfortable in crowds. She is intelligent, as are all Asperger's cases. Yet, her intelligence isn't always as focused as it might be.

We should realize that there are a variety of personality types, a fact which is bound to provoke clashes no matter what we do.

ONE PERSON'S "TRASH TALK" is another person's "I just tell it like it is." It's all a matter of perspective. If we put ourselves in the shoes of a person who somehow offends us, we may find that person didn't intend to hurt us at all. It takes time and effort to think like another person, but it's practical. It can bring peace to our hearts in some situations.

Dehumanizing language doesn't always have to involve foul language, yelling, name calling, or other examples of anger. Any pessimistic words that make a person feel like they need to defend themselves can be defined as "trash talk". Some people are sensitive, so it takes very little to make them feel disrespected. Other individuals have thicker skins.

I subscribe to the four-personality theory well-known in certain circles for decades. Usually, people are a combination of personality types, with one dominant personality trait:

- Extroverted, fast-paced, short-tempered, organized, and controlling
- Extroverted, loud, talkative, fast-paced, disorganized, short-tempered, fun-loving, and easy-going
- Introverted, overly analytical, detail-oriented, slow-paced, slow-simmer type of temper, quiet, prone to fear, craves peace
- Introverted, quiet, passive, slow-paced, slow-simmer type of temper, craves peace, prone to fear, and prone to procrastination.

Again, it's important to note each individual's personality will normally be a unique combination of two or more of the four personality types listed above. For example, I know outgoing individuals who are also analytical. I know extroverted people who can be slow-paced and quiet in some situations as well. There are numerous possible combinations of characteristics; that's what makes every person special:

- **Jose and Sylvia** - are prime examples of the maxim "opposites attract". Jose is easy going and carefree. He is unmotivated and disorganized in many areas. On the other hand, Sylvia is intensely emotional and detail oriented. She is always trying to light a fire under her husband to get him to exercise more, care more about his grooming, do more household chores, and spend more quality time with the family. All of Sylvia's nagging doesn't work. The more she pushes, the more her passive-aggressive husband pushes back. Jose seems to be willing to take on more responsibility around the house only during the times when his wife has stopped pushing him.

- *Wife Swap* - is the reality show I mentioned earlier. This series is always a perfect example of the fact that people come in various shapes, sizes, colors, and personality types. The wives can be easy going or strict, loud or reserved, hard working or indolent, messy or obsessively neat, spiritual or uninterested in religion, sports minded or delicate, obsessed by their appearance or uncaring of their appearance, hot tempered or even tempered, spendthrift or thrifty...The list goes on.

    On one of the latest episodes, Trisha, an ultra-feminine, reserved lady traded places with Sheila, a generously-sized, sports-obsessed, outgoing woman. The reserved, delicate lady showed her personality by rarely showing high emotion, having a hard time easing into the other wife's main hobby, speaking softly, putting her heart into her work, and caring about her appearance.

    The outgoing, muscle-bound lady showed her temperament by playing juvenile pranks on everyone, easing gracefully into her temporary career, speaking loudly, not caring about her appearance, not cleaning her own house, and following her own agenda.

    Both of these ladies had hearts of gold, and both of these ladies were able to effect some permanent changes in their temporary families. However, their surface personalities differed greatly.

- **Karinna** - is a tough lady. She has led a difficult life in almost every way imaginable. She has the hide of a rhinoceros. Also, she is an abrasive person. She always tells the bare truth as she sees it, with no modification. Karinna is a font of unsolicited advice, criticism, and undesirable reminiscences. She rarely takes thought for how her thoughtless words will come across to her listener, whether other people want to hear her opinion, or what the consequences of always speaking the facts--as she understands them--will be. In fact, she doesn't stop giving advice and opinions even when she's making her listeners angry.

  In a nutshell, she is the type of person who easily gives offense. However, once you get past the abrasive exterior, you find a heart of gold. It is the heart of a woman who has sacrificed everything for her family over the decades.

  She acts the way she does, and talks the way she talks, because she truly believes she's helping people. For instance, she believes giving negative feedback to people will inspire them to fix what is, in her opinion, broken. Unfortunately, **critical feedback is usually a poor motivator**. The truth is some people don't want to be fixed, or changed. Everyone has different priorities.

- **Sonya** - almost severed ties with me because of my disrespectful communication to her. I wrote her a letter in which I gave my unvarnished opinion on a certain matter. I used no foul language and made no derogatory comments about her. I wrote the message in poor judgment, and in haste, because I was frustrated by years of not having my wishes respected. On her end, Sonya felt personally attacked by my letter.

  One drama-filled phone call and hours of letter writing later, the rift in our relationship was healed. We both learned a lot by metaphorically walking in each other's shoes. Sonya could understand why I was frustrated because she had ignored my wishes for years. For my part, I could easily see why she was offended by my initial, careless letter.

- **Crystal** - refuses to filter anything that comes out of her mouth the same as Karinna. She doesn't use foul language. However, she doesn't think before she speaks. She hasn't mastered the technique of slowing her thoughts down and organizing them before she communicates. She gives unsolicited advice and opinions constantly, and they are rarely delivered in a diplomatic way. She doesn't care, or perhaps she doesn't understand, how strongly her words come across. Crystal shares too much information about her domestic and medical difficulties. Speaking to this lady often makes me feel uncomfortable and anxious.

- **Sarah** - is one of those people who consider compliments to be unnecessary. Like many others, she likes to "inspire" people through "constructive criticism". For example, I was recently working on a project that was important to me. It had taken up a lot of my time and energy for almost two years. I asked Sarah to give me her general opinion on my project. She complied. Her judgment consisted solely of suggestions for improvement. She didn't give me one compliment. I was left wondering why she wanted to continue to look at my project if she didn't find anything of value in it.

Some people don't realize the immeasurable positive impact of even the briefest of compliments sandwiched in the middle of tips for progress.

- **LOREN** IS ANOTHER LADY who consistently refuses to keep her advice and opinions to herself. She is not trying to be offensive. She just sees it as her duty to correct everybody, even when they don't agree with her point of view. She craves immediate transformations according to her desires. She visited her son, Don, recently. He got angry with her because she often pointed out repairs she felt were necessary to his house. She wanted the repairs to be done her way right away. She wouldn't accept Don's lack of desire to do her bidding. The more she obsessively insisted that repairs be done, the angrier her son got. Unsurprisingly, he didn't accomplish any of the repairs she suggested.

Loren isn't trying to demean anyone. She just refuses to accept other peoples' lack of willingness to do her bidding. To her way of thinking, she's doing everyone a favor by determinedly pointing out how things need to be "fixed". The problem is nobody wants her constant negative opinions and advice. Most people would much rather hear positive feedback. **Positive feedback is a motivator; negative feedback isn't.**

Some people refuse to think before they speak and act. These individuals may seem to be continually looking for targets to verbally confront. We shouldn't take anything they say as an attack against us personally. Numerous manifestations of this phenomena can be found in everyday life: road rage; customers who yell at slow cashiers in check-out lines; strangers who give unsolicited advice on how someone should reign in their young children, and; people who give their opinions on how others are dressing and acting.

- **Casey** is a lady I read about in a blog post. She is a sales representative for a direct-marketing company that sales a variety of products. On a specific occasion, she was a customer in the workplace of a teenager. She noticed the teenager had a condition of the skin that may be alleviated by some of her products. Bluntly, she pointed out the ailment, gave the minimum-wage earning teenager a business card, and suggested that he buy her products. The teenager was devastated. I'm guessing he wouldn't have bought anything from Casey even if he could afford to do so. Nobody wants to buy something from a person who has diminished them in any way.

Chapter 6

The Importance of Open Communication (Trash Talk may be the result of simple miscommunication)

True communication is an art. It's never one-sided, or rushed.

IN OUR FAST-PACED SOCIETY, the art of leisurely, mind-sharing conversation seems to be on the endangered species list. Some individuals seem to want to communicate as succinctly as possible. For obvious reasons, hasty, unfiltered communication can be unclear.

Through no fault of our own, we probably won't be understood, or liked, by every person of our acquaintance.

I'VE HEARD MOTIVATIONAL SPEAKERS state that anywhere from 10% to 25% of the people with whom we interact won't like us.

No matter what we do, some people may have personalities that just don't gel well with our own personality. These personality clashes aren't always someone's fault; sometimes they just happen. It's human nature to get along better with some people than we do with other people.

Certain individuals are open about sharing their thoughts and feelings, and others aren't. I am, generally, a reserved person. I open up only to people with whom I feel comfortable. I have found that more outgoing personalities can be confused about what I'm trying to communicate, or how I'm feeling. Some outgoing people can even take personal offense if a reserved person doesn't open up to them immediately. If people are confused by somebody's actions, they probably aren't going to want to interact with that person; it's too much trouble.

Some individuals speak loudly, while others don't. People with more outgoing personalities often have a hard time speaking with an "inside voice" as any caregiver of young children would characterize "speaking softly". Therefore, some people might think more gregarious personality types are yelling at them when disrespect is not their intention. The more outgoing a person is, the more loudly that person may speak. On the reverse side, reserved people usually speak softly.

Miscommunication may be the result of a language barrier.

- **DANIELLE –** IS NOT A native English speaker. She has a limited vocabulary in English. She speaks English rapidly, with a thick accent. She also has a significant hearing loss. Danielle has chosen not to invest in hearing aids because she is living on a limited income. When this lady and I speak, we constantly miscommunicate. We both have hearing losses, so we often have to repeat ourselves. I have lost count of the number of times during a day we ask each other to repeat what was just spoken. Also, this lady often needs certain complicated concepts repeated five to six times, escalating the level of clarity, and conciseness, each time. Should either of us take the simple miscommunication as a personal affront? Probably not.

- **Naomi -** is an example of how even fluent non-native speakers of English may struggle with idiomatic language. It's easy to get confused when you don't understand the subtle nuances of words in their language of origin. Naomi is the chorister for a local church's kids' church auxiliary. Recently, Terry, the pianist that works with her, notified Naomi that a certain activity Naomi planned was a little confusing for her. Terry didn't criticize the chorister, or the activity. In fact, the pianist complimented her on choosing the fun activity before suggesting a minor change.

The result of the communication was that the chorister said she would try to be more thoughtful, and she was sorry for giving the pianist so much trouble. The chorister's words were confusing to the native-speaking pianist. In English, the words "giving you so much trouble" have the connotation of referring to a huge problem, not a minor conflict. Terry was picturing Naomi feeling chastised, which hadn't been her intention at all.

What is considered to be trash talk to one generation may be considered to be normal conversation by another generation.

PERSONALLY, I FIND THAT the recent trend of super-abbreviated conversations has led to a trend of abrupt, offensive communication. The younger generation seems to expect their easily misunderstood, minimalist language to flow at the speed of light. Amanda shared that her 18-year-old son can barely be bothered to stop whatever he's doing in order to respond courteously to her infrequent conversational gambits.

He often replies to her simple questions with terse answers. The perception of this teenager's mother is that he is deliberately being disrespectful, although that might not be his actual intention.

Some people are naturally brusque in their communication.

IT IS EASY TO get upset by terse people. On the other hand, such individuals might not be trying to hurt other people. They might not realize how offensive their manner of speaking is. I have been told

I am too blunt. Lately, I have been working hard to surround any negative observations I make with appropriate positive observations. This is especially helpful if my listener asks for my candid opinion on something. I have found that most people are much more likely to listen to suggestions if any negative talk is toned down. Also, it's helpful to remember that **people who ask for opinions are often just hoping for validation of their own views.**

A few years ago, the ladies' auxiliary at my church was planning a talent show for Christmas in which they wanted the kids to participate. However, they were only giving the participants two weeks to prepare. Unfortunately, I made my opinion immediately clear by e-mail before I weighed the consequences. I told the organizers of the performance I didn't think they were giving the members of the kids' church time enough to prepare their presentations. I also told them I thought the talent show should be expanded to include all church members.

Nobody had asked for my blunt opinion that seemed to diminish the hard work the ladies' auxiliary was putting into planning the program. I regretted my bluntness immediately. I wrote e-mails apologizing to the organizers of the program.

Some people don't realize how powerful words are.

IN THE EPISODE OF *Wife Swap* I mentioned previously, Trisha cleaned house all day and organized tea parties to teach manners to young girls after school hours. The other wife, Sheila, and her family lived for lifting weights.

Trisha, the lady who was obsessed with manners, immediately started telling Sheila's family what she felt needed to change. She said that lifting weights was not an appropriate sport for young ladies, among other things. She didn't raise her voice, but she didn't tone her words, either. I know that she thought she was helping the family. Yet, what the teenage daughters heard, initially, was "You're wrong to pursue this inappropriate hobby. You disappoint me. You don't meet my high expectations. You're not good enough." I know this because that's the precise message the tearful oldest teenage daughter said she was receiving.

Our brains are complicated. The words we say are not always the exact words that register in our listeners' heads. **Our listeners might not remember our precise words, but they will remember how our words made them feel, perhaps for decades.** In this case, what the girls initially gleaned from the visiting wife's talk was disrespect for the sport that had completely defined them for their whole lives. The temporary mother was trying to help them. In the short term, she ended up hurting them.

Miscommunication can result from non-verbal communication, too.

DIFFERENT SOCIAL OR ETHNIC groups may have their own ideas on what types of gestures, body language, clothing, jewelry, or body decorations are offensive.

A good example of easily misconstrued non-verbal communication is found in the disparate uniforms of Union general, Ulysses S. Grant, and Confederate general, Robert E. Lee, at Appomattox, Virginia, United States, in 1865. Lee surrendered his Army of Northern Virginia to Grant at Appomattox. This signaled the end of the Civil War. Lee was impeccably dressed, as usual. He arrived at Appomattox courthouse in his best Virginia general's full dress uniform. His uniform included his priceless, one-of-a-kind, gold gilt, French-made ceremonial sword. On the other hand, Grant showed up late, direct from the field, in a dusty Union private's field uniform with only shoulder straps to denote his lofty rank. Also, Grant carried no weapon of any kind, which was unusual.

Grant may have had no conscious intention of disrespecting Lee. Grant was reputed to be an inattentive dresser, while Lee was known to be a conscientious, tasteful dresser. Grant may have come dressed the way he did for the sake of convenience, or because he was suffering from a migraine headache (as history records.) Yet, Lee might not have been aware of the mitigating circumstances. Lee may have been offended.

Chapter 7

The Importance of Rejecting Labels and Stereotypes

When people diminish us, they are often focusing on only one aspect of our personality.

IF A DRIVER THAT I have never seen before leans on his horn and yells at me because I cut him off, he is judging me solely on my perceived driving skills at that moment. I may be the kindest, most philanthropic person he is likely to know, but that driver can't see beyond the brief period when I cut him off. We need to remember that people can be selfish and self-centered. We need to learn not to take everything that everybody does personally.

―――――――◦―――――――

Aside from certain authority figures, it is not anyone's job to judge law-abiding citizens.

WE MAY BE GOING THROUGH a life-changing trauma of some sort that is temporarily causing us to make poor decisions. We may have just heard bad news, or we may be in the midst of a challenging illness. For example, my chronic medical condition slows me down and fogs up my brain, as I have already said. I can't count the number of times that people have honked at me, or yelled at me, because I have dared to force them to tap their brakes when they're in traffic, or I have kept them waiting two seconds beyond the time when the stoplight has turned green. If these people knew what I was dealing with, they might have chosen to be a little more patient with me.

ACCEPT NO TRASH TALK

Only people in authority over us have a right to judge us based on only one mistake we might have made during a troublesome time in our lives.

ASIDE FROM CRIMINAL MATTERS, one mistake should not be allowed to completely define a person. Every person is an amalgamation of a lifetime of (wise and foolish) choices and experiences.

If we treat a lifelong friend with grievous disrespect in a certain instance, that friend can choose to not stay offended in order to safeguard a friendship that has lasted decades. On the other hand, that friend can also choose to throw away decades of a nurturing friendship because of the isolated incident of offense.

There is good and bad in almost everyone.

WHEN PEOPLE DISRESPECT US, we may feel that they are concluding there is no good at all in us, which is rarely true. For instance, it's been said that even Al Capone, the most powerful mob boss in Chicago, Illinois, United States, during the 1920's, was kind to some of his close relatives.

A more convincing example of someone who wasn't all bad is Capone's lawyer, "Easy" Eddie Joseph O'Hare. O'Hare was desperately poor before Capone recruited him to be his top lawyer. The two men collaborated in business and law. Little by little, O'Hare got sucked deeper into Capone's empire. As Capone's power grew, O'Hare's power grew. The men became two of the richest, most powerful men in Chicago. However, it seems O'Hare's conscience remained active.

Easy Eddie was instrumental in helping the Internal Revenue Service (IRS) prosecute Capone for tax evasion in 1931. A conviction for tax invasion was the last hope of the Federal Bureau of Investigation (FBI) because Capone bought off too many officials, and hid his tracks too well, to be indicted on any other charges. O'Hare introduced the prosecuting team to the Capone bookkeeper, whose testimony was instrumental to convicting Capone. He also tipped off the prosecuting team that the first jury selected was fixed. Therefore, a new jury was chosen.

Thanks in large part to O'Hare, Capone was convicted. O'Hare was shot, at age 46, on November 8th, 1939, while he was driving his car. It's widely assumed that Capone was behind the execution, although it's never been proven.

The story doesn't end there. The story ends at Chicago's O'Hare airport. Easy Eddie's legacy of fighting for truth and fighting the odds was passed on to his son, Edward Henry "Butch" O'Hare. One of the busiest, most well-known airports in the United States is named after this first-ever Naval Flying Ace who was awarded a Naval Congressional Medal of Honor. Easy Eddie's son was a war hero who almost single handedly saved his own ship, the United States aircraft carrier, USS Lexington, from imminent destruction by Japanese bombers during World War II.

Disrespectful speech facilitates the forming of roots of rejection.

REJECTION IS RARELY ISOLATED to the surface of our emotions. We carry it deep in our emotional make up. In other words, rejection is one emotion that plants roots deep in our psyche:

- **David -** had skin cancer. The skin cancer had progressed to an advanced stage before it was diagnosed. When the cancer was cut out, it had deep, spread-out roots. If David had waited any longer to take care of the cancer, the roots would have grown as far as his eye. He could have lost his eyesight in the affected eye.

- **Bamboo trees** - have a complicated root system. The root system takes about five years to grow. In the meantime, none of the plant is visible above ground. However, after five years, the root system is sufficiently developed to allow the plant itself to grow above the ground. In that first year of growth (of the plant itself), the bamboo tree can shoot up dozens of feet.

It's clear that, if we don't want to cause deep damage to our psyche, we mustn't allow rejection to take root in our minds. Whatever affects our minds affects our bodies. That's a widely accepted scientific fact.

We shouldn't feel the need to worry about the good opinion of people who we're likely to lose track of within the next five to ten years.

PEOPLE MOVE ON AND get new lives. Does it make any sense that we'd trouble ourselves with the good opinion of every person who has a temporary connection with us? I don't even keep in touch with many people with whom I was sure I had formed a lifelong bond, let alone people who marginalized me during my school years. Why would I? Yet, their opinion seemed to matter so much at the time. Why should we allow callous words, spoken in haste by passing acquaintances, to wound us so deeply? It doesn't make any sense, if we look at the big picture.

When everybody's lives have moved on, how important will the earlier disrespect we were shown seem?

Will the feeling of being disrespected be worth carrying with us for an extended period of time? How long do we want to live in darkness, hurting no one but ourselves? Granted, some people are subjected to long-term abuse that may take years to overcome. I'm not trying to minimize that. Thank goodness, some bullying will be less prolonged.

- **Melissa** - told me her 7th grade daughter, Veronica, cried for hours because a popular friend didn't invite her to a party. I don't think the daughter's friend openly bullied her or made a big deal of out of withholding the invitation. Yet, the girl was still devastated by the rejection. Melissa observed this is the sort of heartache we forget soon after we graduate from high school.

How much will this temporary setback mean to Veronica five, or ten, years down the road? By that time, it's possible she may not even remember the name of the friend whose party she wanted to attend. She probably won't remember the hurt that she felt, either.

- **Melissa -** also told me a story that reminds me how **time has a way of whittling down many things that seem large in our minds today, including the opinions of the popular crowd**:

Two of the top football players in her daughter's high school quit college after only a year. Both of them returned home to live with their parents. They hold minimum-wage jobs. Entry-level positions have their place, but they don't provide the financial independence most adults are looking for.

These high-school football stars have gone from being big fish in a little pond to being big fish in a big lake. They're in the real world now. It's safe to assume their words don't hold the power they did in high school. The young men probably don't seem as large as before, metaphorically speaking.

- **Colin -** is a formerly bullied sales associate who was featured on *Undercover Boss*. He worked in a small store that sold print and digital media. Colin went beyond his duties by designating himself a purchasing agent. He would buy whatever print and digital media his research told him were selling well throughout the United States. He would also keep track of which products were selling in his store. Then, he would use that information to prepare his next order. The young man was intelligent, organized, and loyal, among other things. The visiting undercover boss, Tom, immediately determined the employee was underemployed.

The most inspiring aspect of Colin's stellar work ethic was the fact that he was taking on vast responsibilities when he hadn't even completed his high-school education. He had dropped out of high school due to bullying. He got a GED (General Education Development) in lieu of a high-school diploma.

Colin is probably more successful than most of his former bullies. His success is due to the fact that Tom insisted that he go into management training, which would provide a 35% salary increase. In the meantime, I wonder what happened to the people who abused him. Are they earning barely above minimum wage somewhere?

Summary of Reasons
Why We Shouldn't Let Trash Talk Bother Us

THERE ARE MANY SOURCES of negativity in the world today. Manmade and natural trauma are seen everywhere. It is hard to stay positive. However, each person has a right to deflect inappropriate pessimism. The following list of reasons why we shouldn't let trash talk bother us is my personal "go-to" list for times when I feel disrespected:

- We're acceptable as we are, as long as we aren't hurting people or breaking the law.
- Demeaning speech isn't always personal.
- Trash talk is just an unquestioned way of life for some people.
- We should not be judged for that which is beyond our control.
- Internalizing trash talk is unhealthy.
- Bullies are likely to reap the harvest of their negativity at some point.
- Those who judge us may not be aware that we have medical issues limiting our abilities.
- People come in different personality types, and that's acceptable.
- Individuals judge only one aspect of us when they disrespect us.
- Dehumanizing speech helps form roots of rejection.

The main way we can devalue criticism is to remind ourselves that life is in a state of flux these days, particularly in specific areas of the United States. Victims and abusers will probably move on to new social circles, or jobs, within a few years. **Life moves forward, beyond the temporary heartaches of today.**

Chapter 8

How to Diffuse a Trash Talk Situation

IF WE LOOK AT the situation from the offender's point of view, we may get a new perspective.

We may not approve of their action, but we may understand their motivation. For example, the bosses who fired me must have felt that I was a liability to their companies. I was slowing their organizations down and making messes they didn't want to clean up. These supervisors may have felt that I was disrespecting them personally, as well, because I was unwilling and unable to listen to them.

The offender may consider he is having fun. He may not realize he's hurting people. Humor is subjective because individuals define humor in different ways. For example, some people appreciate slapstick comedy such as that performed by Charlie Chaplin and The Three Stooges. Others may enjoy more subtle humor, such as that found in certain British works of comedy.

- **My Family -** In the 1970's, my family and I were having lunch together. Somebody read aloud a children's riddle: "What's purple and rides a white horse?" The answer is "The Lone Grape". Initially, there were only a few polite titters in response to the joke. Then, my late mother started guffawing. She didn't stop for about 10 minutes. By the time she had stopped, the rest of the family was doubled over with laughter as well. So, my mother started laughing again. The laughter went on for about 15 minutes this time. However, my mother was the person who appreciated the pun the most. The bottom line is this: if we're confused, or offended, it might help to ask ourselves if the motivation of the offender was to hurt us, or to have fun.

- **Tanya** is another example of how the definition of humor may vary from person to person. She's a teenager whose first priority in life is fun. She is willing to work hard at school, on *her* terms, because she knows that's the only way that she'll get good grades. However, outside of school, she goes out of her way to entertain herself constantly, or to find the humor in every situation. For example, she loves to bluntly point out every mistake people make. In addition, she finds it amusing when people get physically hurt, or do something socially awkward. In the end, this girl's motivation is not offense, but self-amusement.

- **Morgan Freeman** is an American actor who walks in the shoes of the characters he plays. He stringently researches every role; therefore, he is more able to portray the character accurately. I understand he extensively followed around two public figures he was going to portray in two different films. By the time he had finished shadowing the celebrities, he had mastered even their gestures and mannerisms. He was actually thinking and acting like the men he was portraying. I'm sure such a deep connection allowed the actor to uncover many of the men's deeper motivations.

The average person will not have the capability of delving deep into the psyche of offenders. What the everyday individual may be able to accomplish is a clarification of the main motivation of bullies. Are the aggressors acting out of a desire to fit in with the most powerful group and promote themselves? Are they acting out of personal pain, medical complications, or revenge for obstruction of their agenda?

If we are able to identify the main motivation of the bullying, it may give us a sense of closure. For example, I've been relieved to discover that medical problems were behind much of the bullying to which I've been exposed. That's an explanation, not an excuse.

Medical challenges may be thrust on us. How we treat people in the midst of those medical challenges is a personal choice.

We can remind ourselves that disrespectful speech may be a manifestation of pain.

If people are going through a crisis of some sort, they might not be likely to concern themselves with their words. For instance, patients in distress have been known to get angry with their caregivers. Parents who are fighting might not be aware of the immediate impact their angry words have on their young children. In other words, dehumanizing speech may be a symptom of a deeply-rooted pain.

We can look further than stereotypes.

For example, I recently saw a story about a clash between Kirstie Alley, a current practitioner of Scientology, and another celebrity who is a former member of the religion. Kirstie Alley didn't appreciate the fact that Deirdre, the other lady, was disrespecting her faith.

Many people are quick to point out the variations between faiths, cultures, ethnic groups, political parties, and value systems. It's a fact that there will always be differences. The challenge is to get beyond the familiar stereotypes and make our own assessments of people who are outside of our comfortable social circles.

- **Nelson Mandela -** was an imminent South African statesman He was tried and imprisoned during the dark times of Apartheid (1962-1990). He and Jake, one of his white prison guards, were able to move beyond stereotypes, even though such an attitude went against training. The white prison guards were taught to believe that their black prisoners were sub-human. It followed that the prisoners didn't deserve any respect. Violence against the detainees was commonplace. Mandela had a lot of bitterness against South African white people. His fellow black prisoners had stereotyped white guards as being cruel and inhuman. After some time, Mandela and Jake moved beyond the labels to treat each other with respect. They understood that they were both victims of learned stereotypes.

- **Frank Sinatra**--was an American entertainer. He was best known as a singer. Sinatra was a member of a well-known, diverse group of performers called **"The Rat Pack"** during the mid-20th century, which included a core group of the A-listers of the time: Dean Martin, Sammy Davis, Jr., Peter Lawford, and Joey Bishop.

   Numerous sources cite Sinatra's kindness to his African-American Rat Pack comrade, Sammy Davis, Jr. For example: when the friends were playing Las Vegas, where Sinatra had a lot of clout, Sinatra wouldn't allow Sammy Davis, Jr. to be treated with disrespect. Sinatra insisted his fellow singer be allowed to eat in the same hotels as the white members of the group. This was a brave step for Sinatra to take in an era of rampant racial disparity and discrimination.

We should remember that people are complicated. Humans can't always be pigeonholed into well-ordered categories.

THERE ARE LIKELY TO be malevolent, selfish people in every crowd. However, that doesn't give anybody the right to judge a whole law-abiding group by a few wayward members. Typecasting is easy, but counterproductive. What if Nelson Mandela and his white prison guard had refused to look beyond labels?

We shoot ourselves in the foot if we deny ourselves access to full knowledge of people who are different from us. It's a good idea to consider our actions well before we jump into judging a person. People are not just labels.

We should recall that people have a right to make their own choices.

ACCEPT NO TRASH TALK

THE WAY THAT WE communicate is a choice. We shouldn't expect to take responsibility for other people's poor choices. In the end, we have the option of not reacting to other people's unwise selections. That means that we have the option of not reacting to others' demeaning communication.

Individuals cannot be controlled, only guided. People have a right to exercise free will. **We cannot control people's actions and attitudes, but we can control our reactions to them**. So, why should we even bother trying to control people? I am sure that I'm far from the only parent whose children don't always do what they're expected to do immediately. Many parents have found that even minor children must be allowed a certain amount of leeway in their choice of hobbies, interests, and attitudes.

As stated earlier, my children's interests do not lie in the area of sports. Their strengths are music, academics, and electronics. Both of my children make their preferences clear. They are both incredibly strong-willed. I don't try to guide their hobbies at this point. I am not a big fan of wasting my own time. I allow them to explore their own interests. They are often slow to do what I expect of them because they are working on their hobbies. I must pick and choose my battles. I don't always win the battles, but I can win the war if I refuse to let their attitudes bother me.

Numerous people will do what they want to do, regardless of the consequences. This phenomenon can be related to health issues. Medical facilities are full of people who refuse to stop eating and drinking too much, taking medications and drugs they shouldn't be taking, or smoking too much. Health-care facilities are full of patients who ignore professional warnings. Sometimes, even people who have the resources to get regular medical care ignore the need to do so.

Some people go for years ignoring the symptoms of serious conditions that need to be addressed.

ALLY SUFFERED MULTIPLE PATHOLOGICAL symptoms for decades. Finally, she took the initiative and tested positive for diabetes. She was used to eating whatever she wanted, as much as she wanted. This caused constant intestinal distress, skin problems, and obesity.

In more extreme examples, I have watched many episodes of a medical reality show, *Dr. G Medical Examiner*, in which some people die because they ignore symptoms of diabetes, severe depression, and intestinal blockage as well as kidney, heart, and liver disease.

The phenomenon of people doing what they want to do, regardless of the consequences, can also be related to trash talk. Some people sabotage important relationships through dehumanizing communication. Some people aren't motivated to change even when they've lost their jobs, families, homes, and even their health. For example: Donna is a lady who made the choice to spread rumors about certain relatives for a period of years. The unsurprising result of this was broken family and business relationships. Family members to whom she had previously been emotionally close chose to distance themselves from her. These relationships will never be completely healed. There will always be an emotional disconnect.

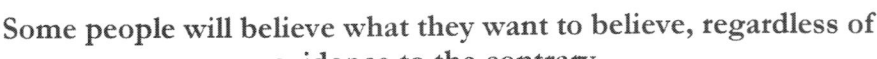

Some people will believe what they want to believe, regardless of evidence to the contrary.

NO AMOUNT OF ARGUING the numbers, data, statistics, or other facts, is going to change their minds. Certain individuals will change their minds when they're ready, not before. Why should we waste our time and energy trying to convert a person to our way of thinking before she's ready to listen? This desire to keep the status quo can relate to religion, health, politics, or personality characteristics.

- **Donna -** Her parents have always kept up hope that their daughter will change. I am not as optimistic as her parents. I haven't seen this lady make a permanent positive transition in the decades I've known her. I still see her treat her parents disrespectfully. For instance, she ignores her aging parents' desires to keep in touch for months on end. The evidence shows that Donna only improves intermittently as it suits her agenda. Yet, her parents never seem to stop believing in her.

- **Frank** - Some parents are faced with the hard truth that their children may make unwise decisions leading to disastrous consequences. Caleb and Mary raised all of their children to live responsibly and be good citizens. Most of their children have chosen to follow the path of being productive members of society. However, one of their children, Frank, followed a path of self-destruction. Frank had mental issues from childhood. He was completely rebellious by the time he became a teenager. Although intelligent, Frank dropped out of high school and fell in with the wrong crowd. This decision led him into a life of crime. He ended up in prison. Luckily, this story has a happy ending: Frank completed his GED in prison. He has also been working on getting certified in a trade that will ensure him a steady, well-paying career.

We may be able to distance ourselves from certain toxic situations, or people, in an honorable manner.

WE CAN EASILY HANG up on people who are yelling at us on the phone. I have no problem hanging up on automated messages, or scam callers. A person can often block, or ignore, people who are offending them on social media. We usually are able to choose our friends in real life; we can choose our friends in cyberspace, too. In addition, we might be able to limit face-to-face interaction with some of our tormenters.

- **Vicky** - attends a small neighborhood church. There is a group of people in her church who she says are toxic. These are individuals she believes have spread gossip about her and others. These ladies don't just pass along cute, amusing stories about people. They spread malicious gossip that can seriously damage a person's reputation. They are also a constant font of emotionally draining stories about their own lives. For the sake of her own sanity, Vicky has chosen to limit her social interaction with these ladies who love to gossip.

- **Sam** - attended church with some wealthy young people when he was a college student. He was poor. He was attending college on a scholarship. Because Sam didn't have much money, he was marginalized in his church of choice. This hard worker was actively ostracized by indolent, proud, selfish young people whose college educations were being financed by their wealthy parents. Sam chose to distance himself from the drama. He transferred to a different church. The new church that he chose was full of humble people. Sam was accepted at once.

We can glory in our own strengths and weaknesses.

WE SHOULD STOP COMPARING ourselves to other people. Diversity can add a necessary spice to life. For example, if the world were full of only skilled performers, teachers, or construction workers, then how would we accomplish engineering and scientific marvels? Where would the Einsteins and the Curies be? **Everyone's capabilities and talents are useful.**

Kelly is a concert pianist. She is also a teacher of advanced piano students and piano teachers. I play the piano a little, but I am not in her league. Unlike me, she has decades of musical-performance experience. However, I have decades of experience in teaching. I have also been writing, for my own enjoyment, for most of my life. While my friend is a superior musician, I may trump her in the areas of teaching and writing.

If someone were to disrespect my musical ability, I could choose not to be offended and remind myself I have other strengths. I could accept the fact that I am not a concert pianist. I don't need to be the best at everything I do. In fact, it's not possible for me to pressure myself to be the best at everything I do without adversely affecting my health.

If we are more accepting of ourselves, dehumanizing speech might not continue to be an issue.

We can choose not to be offended.

IN TODAY'S SOCIETY, MANY people are quick to feel slighted. We still feel demeaned by outright criticism. However, it seems that the list of what's labeled as offensive has recently grown to epic proportion. A few examples follow: locking eyes with an unknown child in public, touching a person in any way without asking permission, rolling our eyes at someone, and raising our voice slightly during conversation.

- **Armand** - His workplace requires sexual-harassment training several times a year. The training is required because his colleagues are quick to sue people over what they perceive to be troublesome non-verbal communication. Armand has become so paranoid about his communication being misconstrued that he chooses to be uncharacteristically subdued around many of his co-workers.

We might sense offenses where none were meant. There are many examples of people who choose to feel demeaned because they believe that they were fired from their jobs due to their race, or religion. The truth is that many of these people may have been fired because of incompetence.

Getting offended is a choice. The healthy choice is to choose not to be offended. We can choose to divorce our ego from the dehumanizing situation.

- **Andrew Carnegie** - was an American entrepreneur at the end of the 19th century. He was able to divorce his ego from traumatic situations and move on. He did not hold pity parties, or wallow in anger. He chose to make lemonade out of lemons. Andrew Carnegie apprenticed to one of the top railroad magnates in the country. Over time, he rose to the top in that industry. However, that's not how Carnegie is best remembered today. When the railroad industry slowed down, Carnegie reinvented himself as the most successful steel magnate in the country, worth dozens of billions of dollars in today's money. This was risky because steel was a costly and untested metal at that time. It had only been used for small parts and jewelry. However, Carnegie didn't let that stop him. He knew steel was the wave of the future. He became best known for steel architecture, such as buildings and bridges.

- **Henry Ford--**was the pioneer of the automobile assembly line in the United States. He also had to fight against tremendous odds. Ford was the first to design and manufacture a car that was affordable for the working class. He had to go to court to win the right to sell his cars independently. He was battling a monopoly of car manufacturers called The Association of Licensed Automobile Manufacturers, which actually owned a patent on the idea of the automobile. This conglomerate had the power to choose who could sell cars, and they refused to grant Ford permission to sell his cars. Still, the entrepreneur refused to give up. He took the powerful conglomerate to court and won the right to manufacture and sell automobiles independently.

We can choose to forgive our offender for the sake of our health.

I'M NOT SAYING THE road will be easy. Obviously, there are some cases in which immediately forgiving someone who has wronged us may be impractical. However, if the option of forgiveness is feasible, we should take it. **Forgiveness often benefits the person that is doing the forgiving more than it benefits the person that is being forgiven.**

Just as internalizing trash talk can be unhealthy, bitterness is unhealthy. Resentment is a catalyst to stress. On the other hand, medical research suggests that letting go of bitterness can reduce stress.

When we reduce tension, we reduce the possibility of disease in the mind and the body. Mercy can help to keep a person's mind free from the darkness that bitterness can bring. The offending person may not perceive any immediate adverse circumstances in his own life. He may remain unaffected and uncaring. However, if the victim is still able to let go of the offense for his own sake, he won't derail himself from the tracks of mental and physical health. For example, the victim may be able to stop ulcers, depression, chronic anxiety, addictions, high blood pressure, intestinal distress, and a myriad of other ailments.

Isn't staying healthy more important than reliving the past? To quote a popular maxim: If we don't have our health, what *do* we have?

YOU CAN TRUST THAT I know what I'm talking about. I have always been the type of person who internalizes any kind of trauma. I've heard it said that every person, or every personality type, has a particular section of the body which is more prone to disease.

It seems my body's most vulnerable sections are my sinuses and my intestines. Therefore, it makes sense that I have decades of trauma internalized mainly in my sinuses and intestines.

Forgiveness is a difficult, but healthy, option to choose when people that are close to us traumatize us.

WHAT MAY MAKE TOLERANCE easier is the reminder that not everybody operates at a mentally stable, socially acceptable level. For instance, Debbie is a public figure whose father, Bruce, abused her in unspeakable ways for the majority of her childhood while her mentally ill mother, Cybil, did nothing. In fact, Cybil allowed Bruce to abuse her, too.

Unsurprisingly, Debbie had to work hard to overcome her deep root of bitterness. She had to come a long way to accepting the fact that her parents didn't love her. More to the point, I would say her parents were unable to love her.

Before he died, Debbie's father tearfully apologized to her. Bruce said he didn't realize what he was doing was wrong until the last years of his life. He didn't know how much he had hurt his own daughter. He was only mirroring the behavior he saw during his own childhood. As for Cybil, she is likely to be dealing with mental issues for the rest of her life. She will never operate at full mental capacity.

We cannot choose people's actions, but we can choose how we react to them.

HURTFUL ACTIONS AREN'T ALWAYS personal against the victim. They may stem from the selfishness, pain, or illness, of the abuser.

Another reason to choose forgiveness is that the offender may have done what they did in ignorance.

THE OFFENSE MIGHT NOT have been given in a spirit of maliciousness. I will use my own parents as a case study: I believe their thinking was clouded due to certain physical and emotional limitations. My parents were doing the best they could, and they thought they were doing the right thing. They loved me to the best of their ability and provided for me. They raised me to treat people right. According to their way of thinking, they were just and fair in their expectations and treatment of me.

Also, I cannot resent the fact that my parents didn't stop me from eating gluten because they were uninformed about the disease of gluten intolerance.

ACCEPT NO TRASH TALK

It's easier to choose forgiveness if we look at the big picture.

WE MAY FIND THAT forgiveness should be an easy choice because **some challenges may, eventually, move us to a higher level of self-awareness and performance**. The deeper we're pushed down through our struggles, the harder we work to push up beyond our struggles. Work of any kind makes anybody stronger in the long term.

People who aren't willing to work hard may not go as far in life as individuals who swim upstream against struggles. This phenomenon is illustrated in the case studies of real-life celebrities I mentioned earlier in the book.

I do not presume to put myself on the same level as celebrities except for the fact that I have had to overcome challenges. I am a stronger person because of the challenges I've had throughout my life.

The Story Trek is a reality shows that features inspiring and unusual stories from across America. One episode featured Carla, a reigning beauty queen who was subject to violent abuse during her middle-school years. She was bullied in person and online. However, when the once-devalued young lady went to high school, she blossomed. She became popular, and she excelled in dance. Since she has become a beauty queen, she has traveled to many places throughout the United States to talk to kids about bullying. She is a prime example of a person of excellence who is using her pain to connect with other people.

Here's a perspective that we don't hear every day: **Our challenges may be our future friends in disguise; they can teach us about ourselves**. Trials can help us rise to the next level. They can help us to rise out of fear and obscurity. Therefore, our challenges may even be our mentors in disguise. However, we probably aren't going to have that mindset when we're in the middle of traumatic times. Wisdom may come later.

Summary of Ways to Diffuse a Trash Talk Situation

THERE ARE A VARIETY of methods I have found to be helpful in diffusing a disrespectful situation. People I know have found these methods to be useful as well, although they are not proven solutions for every situation:

- Analyze the offender's motivation. Are they driven by malevolence? Are they driven by a simple desire only to amuse themselves? Or, are they driven by the trauma and wrong thought patterns caused by their own pain?
- Ask ourselves if the offender's medical concerns are the catalyst to the trash talk.
- Move beyond the stereotypes that society perpetuates.
- Refuse to accept responsibility for others' poor choices.
- Distance ourselves from toxicity where possible.
- Become more comfortable with our own strengths and weaknesses.
- Choose not to be offended.
- Choose to forgive the offender for the sake of our own health.

Chapter 9

Why We Need to Set Up Emotional Boundaries

IN ORDER TO KEEP ourselves mentally strong enough to deflect trash talk, we need to set up emotional boundaries.

It's common that people bully those people whose defenses, or boundaries, they characterize as weak.

- Bosses might harass subordinate workers.
- Young people might bully elderly people.
- Cruel individuals may bully gentle people.
- Members of the majority race, or religion, in a certain geographical area may demean people of other races and religions.
- Athletes might harass those they consider weak.

The boundaries we can set up include the following:

Disconnect from bullies in cyberspace

In this information age, devaluing communication can happen to anybody, anytime. Cyberbullying is a new word coined in the last few years because people have become more connected, in real time, through the internet. There are often stories in the news of even preteens who are completely devastated because they are cyberbullied by their peers. The fact that mere words in cyberspace cause some traumatized teens to want to switch schools points out the importance of words. In online confrontations, no physical violence is involved, only words.

A word has been created to describe people who post negative comments on sites and posts: "troll". I have seen the traumatic effects of trolls' words as they launch personal attacks. Even though the offender's language is usually juvenile, their victims take the demeaning message seriously. Disrespectful language is especially prevalent when the subject under discussion is politics or religion. Dan was a troll who called Cindy "deluded" and "baby sucking a pacifier", among other things, on a particular post. Needless to say, Dan was blocked by the owner of the post. Some people are so disenchanted they don't regularly use social media.

The importance of words cannot be overstated. **Words have real power.**

Disconnect from people who bully us on the phone

I HAVE BEEN CUSSED at, yelled at, and rushed impatiently through one scam spiel after another. When telemarketers get clued in to the fact that I am not going to give them any information, or money, they immediately hang up. I've had telemarketers, and solicitors for charities, yell at me as well. That's a form of bullying.

- **"The Fire Department"**--About seven years ago, a man called asking for donations. He claimed to be from "the fire department", which is a suspicious, general way to identify oneself. He gave no further identifying information. I was trying to eat my dinner. I ended our phone calls twice, and he still called again. When I finally interrupted him on the third phone call, and wouldn't let him get a word in edgewise, he began yelling at me. At that point, I did not feel guilty about hanging up on him.

- **"Windows Tech Support"**--My husband and I recently received three phone calls from one company. The company was listed as "Unavailable" on the Caller I.D. display, but I was curious enough to pick up the phone. Each time, a young man greeted me and said that he was with "Windows Tech Support." This company is non-existent. That was the first red flag.

Windows is a computer software product manufactured by Microsoft Corporation. It is not a separate company. It is not supported outside of the company that created it, Microsoft, without a support contract from a third-party company. When my husband stayed on the phone long enough to see what the scam was, he found that the scammer wouldn't divulge his true company affiliation. That was the second red flag. The man claimed that he would help with a non-existent computer problem if my husband would pay him money.

My husband works in the computer field; he didn't fall for the scam. But, when he went online to research that type of phone call, he found that many people did fall for the scam. Many people pay good money to get their non-existent problem fixed. They're bamboozled by fast-talking "experts" in any field.

- **"Department of the Treasury"**--Recently, I received a call from an unidentified man who stated that he was from the U. S. Department of the Treasury. He said I owed back taxes due to a miscalculation on a previous tax return. The man had no information that a legitimate collection, or government, agency would have. For instance, he only had my address listed correctly. He didn't have my social security number or birth date. He threatened me with arrest, in handcuffs, within a half hour if I didn't pay him immediately. He also suggested that I would receive a prison term of at least two years (before I even went to trial!).

There a multitude of problems with this scenario. It's common knowledge the U.S government moves like a snail. They are all about paperwork. They **do not** have the time, patience, or manpower to make calls. If someone owes them money, they will send letters. The Department of the Treasury is not a law-enforcement agency. They don't have the power to threaten anybody with immediate arrest. Aside from that, nobody is imprisoned permanently in America without a trial.

My other concern with the phone call relates to the phone number itself: My caller identification (I.D.) showed the phone call didn't originate in the "202" area code, the area code of Washington D.C. and most national government offices.

I don't think yelling at someone is an effective method to get that person to buy your product, listen to your cause, or otherwise give you what you want on a permanent, life-changing basis. Perhaps we should ask ourselves the following questions: why do some of us put up with much more disrespect through electronic devices than we would in person? Why do we allow ourselves fewer boundaries when we aren't directly interacting with people?

Most of us wouldn't think twice about at least trying to stop verbal harassment in face-to-face situations, if we had the ability to do so. Perhaps we need to work on expanding our social boundaries to include electronic devices.

Extricate ourselves from demeaning situations

SOMETIMES, INDIVIDUALS ARE BULLIED because they allow it. Some people may choose not to change their traumatic situations because they don't think they're worthy of being treated within the boundaries of polite society. Other persons may choose to socialize only with people who respect them, walk away from potentially explosive situations, or get a new job. **Every person is worthy to take the option of disconnecting from drama.**

We may refuse to form a bond with people whose views don't agree with our own. Dana has been de-friended by some Facebook friends because they were offended by her conservative, religious postings. Dana has also de-friended some of her Facebook friends because they posted foul-mouthed tirades against certain groups and individuals on their own Facebook pages.

Don't try to socialize with the most popular crowd if that crowd won't accept us as we are (Why should we want to be part of a group that devalues us?)

- **Alisha** - was romantically interested in a handsome, popular young man, Diego, during her college years. This man was not interested in her. He didn't want her to be a part of his group. The more

Alisha tried to befriend Diego, the more callous he became. In the end, the young man felt that he had no option but to say some rude words to Alisha so that she would leave him alone. His cruel words have haunted the lady for some time.

- **Jenny--**is on the opposite end of the spectrum from Alisha. She was part of the respected group when she attended college. She was a certified genius, gorgeous, talented, and wealthy. Jenny knew how to wear cosmetics and dress to her best advantage. Ben wanted to date her. He was not popular, wealthy, handsome, or intelligent. He was slovenly and financially challenged. He didn't take care of his body. Frankly speaking, he was not in Jenny's league. The young woman immediately turned down his offer of a date without a qualm. Ben may have had sterling personality characteristics, but Jenny didn't value him enough to find out.

Refuse to allow anybody to bully us on the job

MICHELLE AND LORI ARE petite ladies who have successfully set up boundaries throughout their lives. They are both teachers, and their students respect them because they know that these ladies value themselves. Michelle and Lori respect their own authority despite their size. They have no problem managing their students. They have total control over their classrooms because they expect to have total control.

It's not hard to live up to our own subconscious expectations. However, it's impossible to exceed our own subconscious expectations.

Summary of the Need for Emotional Boundaries

EMOTIONAL BOUNDARIES ARE CRUCIAL to deflecting bullying and trash talk. In the world of electronics, we can disconnect from aggressors. In the real world, we can try to extricate ourselves from victimizing people and situations. We may also be able to choose to socialize with people who accept us as we are.

Chapter 10

How to Set Up Emotional Boundaries

GIVEN THE FACT THAT we should all consider ourselves worthy to set up emotional boundaries, how can this be accomplished?

Form relationships that empower our uniqueness

We can resist aggressive peer pressure to become a cookie cutter cutout of the accepted group. That may save us from trauma. For instance, I remember being disrespected in high school as I attempted to sit at the lunch table where, Alexis, a popular girl was sitting. I only intended to sit at that table long enough to compliment her on her performance in the recently produced school musical. Alexis wouldn't let me talk. She immediately yelled at me and told me to leave the table. The complicating factor is that I had taken at least one class with Alexis. In that class, we sat at the same table. She had been kind to me. Yet, when she got a starring part in the school musical and became popular, she didn't have any time for me.

I wonder what that young lady is doing today. She was a big fish in a little pond in high school. Yet, she may have completely disappeared off the radar since she graduated. This young lady's status switched from unknown to popular within a matter of weeks. Once the musical closed down, her status probably switched back to unknown within a matter of weeks. It just goes to show how fleeting and meaningless fame can be in any venue. We should all ponder the question of how long we will remember the names of the most popular kids in our high school. For better or for worse, everybody moves on.

Work within our own limitations

ACCEPT NO TRASH TALK

WE CAN ACCEPT THE fact we may not have the desire to rise above certain limits. The truth is we may not be willing to put in the work necessary to rise above certain constraints.

- **Me** - I was not willing to put in the work to rise above some of my own limitations. As stated earlier, I play the piano a little. That is my musical skill. I have decades of experience on the piano. This experience includes taking lessons, practicing at home, and being the pianist for various church groups. On the other hand, I am not gifted in singing, or acting. Every talent and skill must be cultivated. I have never had the time, money, or inclination to take voice or acting lessons. Yet, when I was a student, I ambitiously auditioned for various theater and musical theater productions. I made the final cast of only a handful of high school musicals and college graduate-student productions.

- **Joyce Meyer** - is a Christian minister who I greatly admire. For over three decades, she has studied the Bible and other Christian literature. In exchange, her consistent, voracious research has helped her become one of the most well-known Christian authors and speakers in the world. Her sermons are broadcast on T.V. in many countries. She travels to numerous underprivileged areas. In these locations, Joyce's ministry helps to coordinate practical relief for the inhabitants' immediate health and financial concerns. Joyce concentrates on encouraging the inhabitants through her amazing powers of speech.

    Joyce Meyer is skilled at her two main strengths of writing and speaking, but she allows she is lacking certain other talents. She says that she is not musical, nor is she domestic. She doesn't sing at her own events. Joyce hires people to do that. She doesn't cook, sew, garden, or clean her own house. She hires people to do that. In summary, she has not been able to devote as much time to building musical and domestic skills as she has to building speaking and writing skills. Therefore, she must continue to accept her limitations in the areas of music and domesticity.

- **Cheryl** - is a skilled vocalist. Cheryl has been performing and taking voice lessons for decades. She performs at concerts throughout the area where she lives. Yet, she continues to take voice lessons. She continues to expend time, money, and energy on her vocal talent. Sometimes, she schedules so many performances that she loses her voice. She works daily to expand the limits on her vocal talent. Therefore, her vocal talent is improving daily.

The development of every talent costs in time and money. Nothing happens overnight.

There are no shortcuts to success.

Identify our Strengths

I could have concentrated on improving my academic and piano-playing abilities, instead of my weaker abilities in theater.

I was always an honors student until I got to college. My academic abilities seemed to transfer well into teaching abilities. I have been a substitute teacher for years. I have also taught various classes at my church over the past three decades. My academic abilities seemed to transfer well into writing abilities, too. I have been writing for my own enjoyment for most of my life. As stated earlier, I have also had a chance to hone my piano skills over decades of intermittent piano lessons and volunteer positions in my church.

Summary of How We Can Set Up Emotional Boundaries

SOME INDIVIDUALS MAY RESPECT us more if we work within our own assets and limitations. People may also admire us if we interact with people who have our own social standards.

Chapter II

Conclusion

We can choose what goes into our own minds.

WE CHOOSE WHAT GOES into our minds in the same way as we choose what goes into our bodies. Health-conscious people will limit the amount of harmful substances they allow into their physiques. By the same token, we choose what we allow in our psyches. We have the right to tune out the derogatory comments and tune in to positive self-talk. A good example of this is found in Joyce Meyer and Joel Osteen. They both say they don't listen to their detractors.

Joyce Meyer says she doesn't even allow anyone else to make her aware of her own negative publicity. She filters out the little Tonka™ toy trucks full of undesirable input from her detractors, but she accepts the monster truckloads of positive feedback from thousands of fans.

We should train ourselves to do the same thing: block the negativity, but allow in the positivity.

To further illustrate the need for filtering: Most of us have no problem blocking pessimistic input from electronic devices. We have the option of changing the channel or turning off the device. Why shouldn't we superimpose this same filtering ability onto our brains? Some recent scientific research promotes the theory that our brains are a kind of organic computer. Why should we allow people to dump negativity into our organic computers?

We certainly wouldn't allow people to dump trash into our electronic computers. Such garbage is called "viruses", or "trojans", and we work hard to keep it out.

We can tune out negative people.

WE ARE ALLOWED TO tune out any sort of inappropriate negativity that individuals may throw our way. People may be red–in–the-face raging at us, or people may simply be using a disrespectful tone of voice. Either way, let's think twice before we accept their trash talk. It's also important to revisit two important facts:

- People who yell are only screaming because they feel they've lost control
- Individuals who scream aren't respected; they are only temporarily feared. They have to keep re-instilling that fear every time they yell, because they know of no other way to keep order.

It shouldn't be difficult to tune out immature, out-of-control people. Sometimes, it's hard to take them seriously. I have already stated how I stopped listening to screaming bosses.

- ***Mystery Diners*** - In one episode, Carmen, a cashier was caught stealing food from the owners in order to illegally run her own catering business out of the owners' restaurant. When Carmen was faced with the incriminating evidence, she got defensive, denied criminal intentions, and started calling everything and everybody "stupid". Wisely, her bosses didn't even attempt to respond directly to the juvenile rant. They simply told her she was fired.

- **Alex -** was demanding to use the telephone on the front desk of the office of my college apartment building. Stephanie, the office manager, said she couldn't allow him to do that because she couldn't tie up the business line. Alex, the student, became increasingly angry as the manager continued to deny him access to the telephone. By the time the encounter was nearly over, Alex was screaming at the top of his lungs. His last hurrah, before he stormed out of the office, was to sweep every document off the office's reception desk onto the floor with his hand.

We should feel free to filter out the negativity of people who have a track record of seeing the metaphorical glass as being half empty, instead of half full.

IN OTHER WORDS, THEY choose to focus only on the negative in everything and everybody. The minimal amount of positive feedback that they give is outweighed by the almost constant barrage of negativism.

- **Kim -** is a controlling person. She is much more likely to criticize than compliment. If she does give a compliment, it is almost always overshadowed by her obsession with negative details.

- *Undercover Boss* - In this series, the attitudes of the featured employees vary from angry to indifferent to bubbly. In other words, some of the employees see the glass as half full while other employees see the glass as half empty. All of the featured workers are dealing with personal challenges. Many of the workers are dealing with life-altering trials. Yet, the top-performing workers choose to remain hopeful against unbelievable odds. At the end of each show, the workers are reprimanded, or rewarded, according to their attitude and work ethic. Obviously, the optimistic employees get more rewards than the pessimistic employees.

We Can Believe in Ourselves.

IT'S ALL ABOUT ATTITUDE. The successful people I've mentioned had every opportunity to indulge in pity parties. Yet, they chose to rise above negativism. We have the same ability. **When we hear pessimistic language, we can counter it with positive self-affirmations.**

We can remind ourselves that any disrespectful speech is probably only addressing a small moment in time, or a small part of our personality. Therefore, the trash talk is skewed. I am reminded of the well-known analogy of the five, or six, blind men who were directed to touch different parts of an elephant. One man was asked to touch the tail, one was asked to explore the ears, and so forth. Every one of the blind men came up with a different description of what sort of animal the elephant might be based solely on his evaluation of the small part of the elephant which he was directed to touch. None of them guessed the animal was an elephant. The point is that none of the participants had the full mental picture of the huge animal they were actually touching. They each only had a small part of the complete picture.

In the same way, we each have a more complete perspective on our own lives than any angry stranger, boss, or co-worker. We have known ourselves our whole lives. We probably know ourselves better than any other person knows us. It follows that we might be the only individuals who are aware of our true worth.

Katy Perry is a popular American vocal artist. Despite her youth, she has been through some trying times in her life. I heard that she, like many other performers, went through many rejections before she found a record label that would sign her on as a vocal artist. Recently, she has also undergone the dissolution of at least two high-profile relationships. Yet, she hasn't allowed any hard knocks to jar her own sense of self-worth. This is evident when we listen to one of her latest hit songs, called "Roar". In a nutshell, the song talks about how Katy Perry is going to break out of her shell and show everyone her newfound strength, especially her past detractors.

Join me in showing the world a lion that roars! Join me in changing the channel on negativism! Let's walk down the road to self-acceptance and self-empowerment together! The journey may be long, but not impossible. The catch is that we must make the journey under our own power. We are responsible for securing our own transportation. Nobody can make the journey in our place. However, people may help us, or hinder us, along the way. If people want to judge us on our inevitable blunders, instead of kindly showing us the most efficient way to move ahead in life, that's their problem. Such people will pay the price for their callousness somewhere down the road. That's The Law of the Harvest that I mentioned earlier. That's another book!

We Can Believe in the Law of the Harvest.

THE LAW OF THE Harvest is a scientific fact. The Law of the Harvest says what is sown must be reaped.

We cannot plant tomatoes and harvest potatoes. It's not scientifically possible. I have seen real examples of this law in social situations as well as in horticulture. I have seen people who are cruel reap the eventual consequences of that spitefulness. We may not personally witness most of our detractors reap a harvest of their negativity. Yet, **we can rest assured there are eventual consequences for every action a person takes; it's an immutable law of the universe.**

- **My Dream -** This dream seemed to send a symbolic message to me: I was returning to college as an older student. I was living in a college dormitory on campus. I was preparing to wash my clothes in the communal laundry room when two tall, handsome, well-dressed, grinning college-aged men entered the room and headed purposefully for me.

  It was obvious the purpose of these young college students was to belittle me. On the surface, they seemed to be preparing to compliment me. Yet, I could sense the conversation was shifting into an amusing (to them) diatribe against what they considered to be my inadequacies. They were going to try to lull me into a false sense of feeling accepted while they prepared to vent their true feelings. I cut them off after about two sentences. I informed them I knew exactly what they were doing, and I wasn't going to stand for it. I continued to lecture them as I chased them out the door and down the street.

Please keep in mind that I was fearlessly chasing two physically strong young men who probably weighed twice my own weight. To me, they represented the many real-life people who I would like to see reap the harvest of the trauma they caused to their victims.

- **Literature** - There are many cases of The Law of the Harvest cited in books. My favorite one comes from a book I read a few years ago. I don't remember the title at this point. It was a memoir of a specific time during Jerome's career. He was a United States government intelligence worker who was mistreated by his supervisor, Wendell, solely because of his religion. In fact, Wendell didn't try to hide the reason for the mistreatment. The book detailed how Jerome was verbally abused at company headquarters in the United States.

  When he was sent to a foreign country, he was ordered by his agency to throw his gun in a river and sent to a long-abandoned safe house that was no longer safe. Jerome was left abandoned and unprotected in the former safe house. He had no money, no food, no weapons, and no way to communicate with his agency. It was later revealed this miserable state of affairs was directly ordered by Wendell.

  When the author was finally able to return to the United States, he witnessed the harvest of his supervisor's vindictiveness. Wendell was immediately suspended from the agency. The author's good harvest was a promotion and a relationship with the lady who eventually became his wife, Sophia. He would not have met Sophia if he hadn't been sidelined by his supervisor. She helped him through some of his most trying times in the foreign country.

Sometimes, the malevolent intentions of bullies end up working in our favor. We may reap a healthy harvest from what appears to be a worthless crop while the bullies may reap an unhealthy harvest from that same crop.

We Can Run Our Own Race.

ONE OF THE MAIN messages I want to get across to the reader is that it's okay to march to a different drum, or run a different race. If people aren't happy with our race, or our musical instrument, that's their problem.

Some of us may get a later start in life, like Colonel Sanders. Some of us may get an earlier start in life, like Katy Perry.

It's not important when, or by what method, we succeed. What's important is that we remain true to the divine guidance that we feel within ourselves. We aren't all meant to be Olympic athletes, but we all have something to contribute to the world. There are many types of races to run. There is something out there for people of all colors, shapes, sizes, personality types, fitness levels, and education levels. We need to follow our own inclinations and strengths. **It doesn't matter if we're on the fast track to somewhere, or the slow track. What matters is that we get to the finish line.**

Derek Redmond is a British athlete who is a great example of running our own race. Derek competed in the track and field events at the 1992 Olympics in Barcelona, Spain. His hamstring was already frail because of prior surgeries. His hamstring completely snapped during the beginning of the 400-meter semi-final race. However, he continued to limp along the track. His dad, Jim Redmond, raced down from his seat, and pushed his way through security guards, in order to walk his son to the finish line. Thousands of misty-eyed spectators cheered Derek on with an extended standing ovation. Official Olympic records state Derek Redmond did not finish the race that day. Yet, in my mind, he finished the race with glory.

Derek Redmond finished his own race. The medalists from that day finished their own race. Do we remember the "winners" as well as we remember the "loser"? We probably don't. Can Derek Redmond really be classified as a "loser"? Not in my book!

Redmond wasn't done amazing the world with his determination. A surgeon told him that he would never be able to play sports again. Redmond didn't listen. He did not pursue track anymore. However, he did choose to play basketball and rugby. As proof of his success, Derek Redmond sent an autographed picture to the surgeon who had warned him that his days of being an athlete were over.

No matter what our pace, we'll still be guided to get to where we need to go. In fact, we may finish the race before impatient people who think that their race supersedes our own.

For example, I see police officers give speeding tickets to at least two drivers every morning as I drive my daughter to school. It's ironic that people who think their time is more important than mine may delay their own schedules through their impatience. I might arrive at the school before they do because they felt that they deserved to shave a few seconds off of their driving time.

That calls to mind the fact that the slow-moving, humble tortoise finished the race before the indolent, arrogant hare in the famous Aesop fable. **Flashy, quick-witted hares do not always win, despite appearances. Often, the race goes to the consistent, dependable tortoises.**

We can accomplish the hard work necessary to run our race.

WE MAY NEED TO exercise patience and fortitude. This holds true for most successful people. Our goals may take more time to accomplish than someone else's goals. Anything worthwhile requires time and effort. Experts in any field did not begin as experts. They make what they do look easy because they have had years of training.

We can't circumvent the need for training and hard work. For example, I have spent many years honing my piano skills. I play the piano at a certain skill level. My skill level improves every time that I practice and perform. I didn't learn overnight. My friend, the concert pianist, took her capabilities to an even higher level. It goes without saying that she has put in a lot more work than I have. She has honed her skills for decades. She is running a different race than I am.

We all choose how much we're willing to work, and what skills and talents we will cultivate. This is illustrated by the fact that a high-school dropout will have a limited number of employment opportunities from which to choose.

His financial success is likely to be limited. On the other hand, a person who continues his education and training beyond high school will have many more employment opportunities open to him. The more education a person has, the more successful he is likely to be.

We can make our own decisions.

EVERYTHING RELATED TO OUR goals is our responsibility alone. We shouldn't let society pigeonhole us. We all have the right to our own way of thinking. Nobody can take that away from us.

Viktor Frankl was a respected psychoanalyst, author, and survivor of Nazi concentration camps during World War II. Viktor Frankl believed that even under the most extreme conditions of bullying imaginable our state of mind is still up to us. He believed and lived that truth. He exemplified a life that moves beyond unimaginable trauma to a place of hope and survival. He didn't survive the death camp, Auschwitz, and two satellite camps of Dachau, by letting negativity overwhelm him. In addition, Frankl didn't endure until 1997 by letting the Nazis dictate how he should feel about himself. He, alone, decided how he would feel about himself.

You are worthy to follow your own chosen path.

DON'T LET THE BIG fish in the little ponds dictate your self-image. They will probably be forced into a huge lake at some point, just like the rest of us. Their power over us is transient.

Here's another point worth pondering: "When writing the story of your life, don't let anyone else hold the pen." The authorship of this quote is uncertain. However, it first appeared in an iconic Harley-Davidson™ motorcycle advertisement.

You can do it!

ACKNOWLEDGEMENTS

THERE AREN'T WORDS ENOUGH to thank my soul mate of 23 years, John, for his untiring encouragement, patience, acceptance, and editorial support. This is one of many situations in which a simple "Thank you!" seems inadequate. His unflagging belief in me through the years is what has enabled me to take on huge projects such as this book.

My children, J.D. and Caitlin, who are much more tech savvy than myself, helped with formatting. Caitlin spent hours helping me wade through complicated format techniques.

Another supporter without whose validation and editing I couldn't have finished this book is Ruth. I don't know how many hours she spent editing a significant portion of this book, but I know that she has spent countless hours uplifting me for decades.

I would also like to thank two other wonderful friends who donated hours of their time to editing portions of my book: Francis and Kelly. They both played a part in validating my book while showing me how to tweak the book to become more accessible to the reader. They showed me connections that I hadn't seen myself. Also, they pointed me in directions of which I had been unaware.

I owe a huge debt of gratitude to three public figures that have influenced my life lately: Joyce Meyer, Joseph Prince, and Joel Osteen. Their books and TV ministries have taught me many important lessons. However, the most significant lesson that I have learned from them is that I am loveable and acceptable as I am. That information is invaluable to every human being. That information is the guiding principle behind this book. It's a dream of mine to someday speak to these great validators of every individual!

ABOUT THE AUTHOR

Traci Lawrence is an author, teacher, freelance editor, and blogger living in the mid-Atlantic region of the United States. Her most passionate writing is motivated by her real-life experience, which includes being devalued and physically limited. That's why she focuses on respectful communication. Traci also incorporates her lifelong love of history and current events into her writing.

Visit Traci's Blog

www.tracisworld.com

Made in the USA
Charleston, SC
13 December 2016